THE AUSTRALIAN

Women's Weekly

good food fast

quick, easy, low-fat food to make you feel great

BAUER

MEDIA GROUP

CONTENTS

The oven temperatures in this book are for conventional ovens; if you have a fan-forced oven, decrease the temperature by 10-20 degrees. A measurement conversion chart appears on the back flap of this book.

FIT WITHOUT FUSS

We all know that exercise is beneficial for us. It makes us feel good, reduces the risk of heart disease, lowers blood pressure, helps control weight, improves posture and helps to prevent osteoporosis. Yet many of us still don't exercise. Why not?

In the past it was thought you had to exercise vigorously for at least 30 minutes three to four times a week to get any benefits. However, this is not the case. Short duration activity, around 10 minutes each, that add up to 30 minutes a day has been shown to help decrease blood pressure, blood cholesterol and body weight. This 30 minutes of accumulated exercise does not have to be vigorous, just at a level where your breathing is a little heavier than usual. And it doesn't need running shoes and bicycle pants; for instance, 30 minutes of gentle activity, such as sweeping the floor or gardening, will use up to 350 kilojoules. If you did this daily, it would add up to 124,000 kilojoules a year, which is the equivalent of 3kg of fat. Perhaps we can't bear the thought of going to a gym with all those toned, tanned bodies; perhaps there's never time for a regular walk around the park; or perhaps, despite our best intentions, we just don't enjoy it enough to maintain an exercise regime. Well, here's the good news: you're probably doing more exercise than you think, just by going about your daily life. And, with very little effort, it's possible to do a whole lot more. The following tips will help you increase your daily level of activity by making a few minor changes to your usual habits.

AT HOME

● See household chores as an opportunity to burn kilojoules rather than just drudgery. Put on some lively music and dust or sweep in time to the beat.

● Mix ingredients by hand instead of using a mixer – it'll take longer, but it's marvellous for hand and arm strength and for relieving stress and frustration.

● Instead of setting the table all at once, walk around the table placing the forks, then walk around again placing the knives, and so forth.

● Don't use your clothes dryer (unless it's raining, of course), peg your washing on the clothes line in the fresh air, bending and stretching with each item.

● When watching television, don't just sit there: circle your feet or jiggle your arms and legs. Don't use the remote control: get up and change the channel or adjust the volume. During ad breaks, walk to the other end of the room or get up and stretch a few times.

● Instead of inviting a friend for coffee, suggest you meet in a nearby park and go for a stroll while catching up with the gossip.

SHOPPING

● Instead of circling the car park looking for that perfect spot, park further away and walk the extra distance – you'll probably get to the shops faster anyway.

● Always walk your shopping trolley back to the store instead of leaving it by your car space.

● Use the stairs rather than lifts or escalators. If you can't find the stairs, walk up the escalator instead of just standing still for the ride.

● In the supermarket, to help keep your arms toned, gently push and pull your trolley backwards and forwards while walking down the aisles. You can also do this while waiting in the checkout queue.

IN THE CAR

● Turn on the radio and tap your hands or bop along to the music.

● A red traffic light is the perfect opportunity to work out a muscle or two: try pelvic-floor exercises, or pushing and pulling on the steering wheel, or squeezing and releasing the wheel with your hands.

AT WORK

● Get off the bus one stop earlier on the way to and from work.

● Get out of the lift one stop before your usual floor and use the stairs. As you grow fitter, gradually increase the number of flights of stairs you walk up.

● Leave some walking shoes at work and take a gentle stroll during your lunch break.

● Go window-shopping – it doesn't cost anything to look and will use up kilojoules.

● Walk further than your usual sandwich shop and find a different place to eat.

● Place your wastepaper bin away from your desk and get up and walk to it when needed.

BREAKFAST

buckwheat pancakes with caramelised banana

PREP + COOK 30 MINUTES (+ REFRIGERATION) SERVES 4

The seeds of the buckwheat plant are ground into the flour that is the essential ingredient in Japanese soba, Russian blini and delicious pancakes such as these.

¼ cup (35g) self-raising flour

¼ cup (35g) buckwheat flour

1 tablespoon caster (superfine) sugar

¼ teaspoon ground cinnamon

1 egg

¾ cup (180ml) skim milk

20g (¾ ounce) butter

¼ cup (50g) brown sugar

4 medium bananas (800g), sliced thickly

2 tablespoons water

1 Sift flours, caster sugar and cinnamon into a medium bowl; gradually whisk in combined egg and milk until smooth. Cover; refrigerate 30 minutes.
2 Meanwhile, melt butter in a large frying pan; add brown sugar; cook, stirring, until sugar is dissolved. Add banana and the water to pan; cook, uncovered, stirring occasionally, about 2 minutes or until banana is caramelised.
3 Pour ¼-cup batter into a heated 20cm (8-inch) non-stick frying pan; cook pancake until browned both sides. Repeat with remaining batter to make a total of four pancakes. Cover to keep warm.
4 Just before serving, halve each pancake; divide pancake halves among serving plates. Spoon banana mixture onto each half, fold to enclose filling; drizzle with any caramel sauce left over from caramelising the bananas.

serving suggestion These pancakes also make a lovely dessert.

These flavour-packed dishes will not only make breakfast the most important meal of the day, but also one of the most enjoyable.

test kitchen tips

Fresh strawberries may be used as a filling instead of caramelised bananas. Dust pancakes with icing sugar before serving, if you like.

mushroom and parsley omelette

PREP + COOK TIME 20 MINUTES SERVES 4

4 eggs
6 egg whites
500g (1 pound) swiss brown mushrooms, sliced thinly
⅓ cup loosely packed coarsely chopped fresh flat-leaf parsley

1 Whisk eggs and egg whites in a medium bowl.
2 Cook mushrooms in a heated non-stick 20cm (8-inch) frying pan, stirring, until tender. Add parsley; transfer to a small bowl.
3 Return pan to heat, add a quarter of the egg mixture; cook, tilting pan, over medium heat until almost set. Place a quarter of the mushroom mixture evenly over half of the omelette; fold omelette over to enclose filling, slide onto serving plate. Repeat with remaining egg and mushroom mixtures to make a total of four omelettes.

Swiss brown mushrooms, also called roman or cremini, are light-to-dark brown in colour with a full-bodied flavour. To store, place them on a tray, in a single layer, covered with damp absorbent paper, and store in an area where cool air can circulate around them.

serving suggestion Serve omelettes with thick slices of toasted sourdough bread.
tip Basil can be substituted for parsley.

nutritional count per serving
▶ 5.6g total fat
▶ 1.6g saturated fat
▶ 560kJ (134 cal)
▶ 2.3g carbohydrate
▶ 16.7g protein
▶ 3.6g fibre

fruit salad with honey yoghurt

PREP TIME 15 MINUTES **SERVES** 4

¾ cup (210g) low-fat yoghurt

2 tablespoons honey

200g (6½ ounces) coarsely chopped pineapple

200g (6½ ounces) coarsely chopped rockmelon

250g (8 ounces) strawberries, halved

250g (8 ounces) blueberries

1 large banana (230g), sliced thinly

2 tablespoons passionfruit pulp

2 teaspoons lime juice

12 fresh mint leaves

1 Combine yoghurt and honey in a small bowl.
2 Just before serving, combine the remaining ingredients in a large bowl; accompany with honey yoghurt.

tips You need only small quantities of pineapple and rockmelon, so buy the smallest fruit you can find. Two passionfruit will supply the right amount of pulp. Honey yoghurt can be made a day ahead; store, covered, in the refrigerator.

nutritional count per serving	
▶ 0.4g total fat	▶ 38.6g carbohydrate
▶ 0.1g saturated fat	▶ 6.2g protein
▶ 819kJ (196 cal)	▶ 5.8g fibre

The word muesli, translated from German as 'mixture', is liberally interpreted by the Swiss as a wholesome flavour-packed combination of cereals, nuts, fruit, and honey or sugar.

low-fat toasted muesli

PREP + COOK TIME 40 MINUTES **MAKES** 1.5KG (12 CUPS)

2 cups (180g) rolled oats

1 cup (100g) triticale flakes

1 cup (60g) unprocessed bran

1½ cups (195g) barley flakes

½ cup (30g) rice flakes

1 cup (110g) rye flakes

¼ cup (60ml) macadamia oil

½ cup (175g) honey

⅓ cup (65g) pepitas (dried pumpkin seeds)

2 tablespoons linseeds

2 tablespoons sunflower seed kernels

1 cup (150g) coarsely chopped dried apricots

1 cup (60g) coarsely chopped dried apples

1 cup (140g) coarsely chopped seeded dried dates

1 cup (160g) sultanas

1 Preheat oven to 180°C/350°F.
2 Combine cereals, oil and honey in a large shallow baking dish. Toast, uncovered, in oven, about 30 minutes or until browned lightly, stirring at least three times during the cooking time. Cool 10 minutes, then stir in remaining ingredients.

serving suggestion Serve with skim milk and stone fruit or berries.
tip Store in an airtight container in the refrigerator for up to 3 months.

nutritional count per ½ cup (60g) serving	
▶ 5.5g total fat	▶ 36g carbohydrate
▶ 0.7g saturated fat	▶ 5.8g protein
▶ 902kJ (216 cal)	▶ 6.2g fibre

There can be few things as comforting or nutritious as a warming bowl of porridge. Here, it's given a natural flavour enhancer with the addition of gently cooked apples that taste of cinnamon.

porridge with apple compote

PREP + COOK TIME 20 MINUTES **SERVES** 4

2 medium apples (300g), unpeeled, sliced thinly

¼ cup (55g) caster (superfine) sugar

¼ teaspoon ground cinnamon

¼ cup (60ml) water

8 dried apricots

1 tablespoon sultanas

1 cup (90g) rolled oats

1 cup (250ml) skim milk

1½ cups (375ml) boiling water

2 tablespoons brown sugar

1 Combine apple with caster sugar, cinnamon and the water in a medium saucepan. Cook, stirring, over low heat until sugar dissolves.

2 Bring apple mixture to the boil, reduce heat; simmer, uncovered, 5 minutes. Add apricots and sultanas; simmer, uncovered, about 5 minutes or until apple is tender.

3 Meanwhile, combine oats, milk and the boiling water in another medium saucepan; bring to the boil. Reduce heat; simmer, uncovered, about 5 minutes or until mixture thickens.

4 Serve porridge with apple compote; sprinkle with brown sugar.

nutritional count per serving
- ▶ 2.1g total fat
- ▶ 0.4g saturated fat
- ▶ 1113kJ (266 cal)
- ▶ 54.9g carbohydrate
- ▶ 5.8g protein
- ▶ 4.8g fibre

test kitchen tip

Any other dried fruit, such as prunes, pears or peaches, could be used instead of the apricots.

grilled mango and ricotta with english muffins

PREP + COOK TIME 15 MINUTES SERVES 4

You need two passionfruit for this recipe.

1 cup (200g) low-fat ricotta

¾ cup (210g) low-fat tropical yoghurt

1 large mango (600g)

2 english muffins

2 tablespoons passionfruit pulp

nutritional count per serving
- ▶ 5.2g total fat
- ▶ 3g saturated fat
- ▶ 1016kJ (243 cal)
- ▶ 33.9g carbohydrate
- ▶ 12.5g protein
- ▶ 4g fibre

1 Whisk ricotta and yoghurt together in a medium bowl until mixture is smooth.
2 Slice cheeks from mangoes; remove skin, cut each cheek in half.
3 Cook mango on a heated oiled grill plate (or grill or barbecue) until browned both sides.
4 Just before serving, split muffins; toast both sides. Place half a muffin on each serving plate; top with ricotta mixture and mango, drizzle with passionfruit pulp.

serving suggestion Drizzle some maple syrup over the mangoes, if extra sweetness is desired.
tip If mangoes are unavailable, you could substitute pineapple.

day-before muffins

PREP + COOK TIME 50 MINUTES (+ REFRIGERATION) SERVES 6

⅔ cup (100g) coarsely chopped dried apricots

½ cup (95g) coarsely chopped dried figs

1⅓ cups (95g) All-Bran breakfast cereal

1½ cups (375ml) skim milk

1¼ cups (275g) firmly packed dark brown sugar

1¼ cups (185g) self-raising flour

½ cup (60g) pecans, chopped coarsely

1 Combine apricot, fig, cereal, milk and sugar in a large bowl; mix well. Cover; refrigerate mixture overnight.

2 Preheat oven to 200°C/400°F. Grease a six-hole (¾-cup/180ml) texas muffin pan.

3 Stir flour and nuts into apricot mixture. Spoon mixture into pan holes; bake about 25 minutes. Serve muffins hot or cold.

serving suggestions Serve with fruit jam or top with dried apricots; dust with sifted icing sugar.
tip Muffins can be frozen for up to 2 months.

nutritional count per serving
▶ 8.6g total fat
▶ 0.7g saturated fat
▶ 2167kJ (518 cal)
▶ 98g carbohydrate
▶ 9.9g protein
▶ 10.5g fibre

test kitchen tip

If you have overnight guests or friends coming for breakfast, prepare the recipe ahead for a breakfast of muffins fresh from the oven! The muffin batter is partially made the day before and refrigerated overnight, needing only a few more minutes of preparation before baking and serving.

rösti with ham and cherry tomatoes

PREP + COOK TIME 40 MINUTES **SERVES** 4

200g (6½ ounces) shaved light ham

4 large potatoes (1.2kg)

1 egg white, beaten lightly

cooking-oil spray

200g (6½ ounces) cherry tomatoes

2 green onions (scallions), trimmed, sliced thinly on the diagonal

1 Preheat oven to 220°C/425°F.

2 Place ham on an oven tray; cook, uncovered, until browned lightly.

3 Meanwhile, peel and coarsely grate potatoes; squeeze out as much excess liquid as possible (see page 112). Combine potato and egg white in a large bowl; divide into eight portions.

4 Spray a heated large non-stick frying pan with cooking-oil; place one portion of potato mixture into pan, flatten with a spatula. Cook over medium heat until lightly browned both sides and cooked through. Repeat with remaining potato portions. Cover rösti to keep warm.

5 Cook tomatoes in the same pan until just beginning to soften. Serve rösti with ham, tomatoes and onion.

tip Wilted baby spinach leaves can also be served with these rösti.

nutritional count per serving
▸ 2.9g total fat
▸ 0.7g saturated fat
▸ 1037kJ (248 cal)
▸ 34.9g carbohydrate
▸ 16.7g protein
▸ 4.9g fibre

LIGHT MEALS

vegetable and red lentil soup

PREP + COOK TIME 30 MINUTES SERVES 6

Used since prehistoric times, lentils are an excellent source of protein, fibre and B vitamins.

2 tablespoons mild curry paste

400g (12½ ounces) canned crushed tomatoes

3 cups (750ml) chicken stock

1 large carrot (180g), chopped finely

2 stalks celery (300g), trimmed, chopped finely

1 medium potato (200g), chopped finely

1 large zucchini (150g), chopped finely

¾ cup (150g) dried red lentils

½ cup (60g) frozen peas

⅓ cup (80ml) light coconut milk

2 tablespoons coarsely chopped fresh coriander leaves (cilantro)

¼ cup fresh coriander leaves, extra

1 Cook curry paste in a heated large saucepan, stirring, about one minute or until fragrant. Add tomatoes, stock, carrot, celery, potato and zucchini; bring to the boil. Reduce heat; simmer, covered, 5 minutes.

2 Add lentils to soup mixture; return to the boil. Reduce heat; simmer, uncovered, about 10 minutes or until lentils are just tender. Add peas; return to the boil. Reduce heat; simmer, uncovered, until peas are just tender.

3 Remove soup from heat; stir in coconut milk and chopped coriander. Sprinkle with coriander leaves just before serving.

serving suggestion Accompany with pappadums puffed in a microwave oven, and a small bowl of raita (finely chopped cucumber combined with low-fat yoghurt).

tip A hotter curry paste or some finely chopped chilli can be added to boost the flavour.

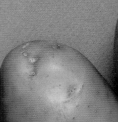

Whether you want a quick lunch or a light supper – or just to keep the munchies at bay in-between meals – this appealing selection of low-fat soups, sandwiches, stir-fries and salads should keep you feeling satisfied.

nutritional count per serving
▶ 4.9g total fat
▶ 1.5g saturated fat
▶ 761kJ (181 cal)
▶ 20.5g carbohydrate
▶ 10.5g protein
▶ 7.9g fibre

pork rice-paper rolls

PREP + COOK TIME 35 MINUTES **SERVES** 4

350g (11 ounces) minced (ground) pork

1 clove garlic, sliced finely

1cm (½-inch) piece fresh ginger (5g), grated

1 teaspoon chinese five-spice powder

350g (11 ounces) finely shredded wombok
(napa cabbage)

4 green onions (scallions), sliced thinly

1 tablespoon soy sauce

¼ cup (60ml) oyster sauce

¼ cup tightly packed, coarsely chopped
fresh coriander leaves (cilantro)

12 x 22cm (9-inch) round rice paper sheets

¼ cup (60ml) sweet chilli sauce

2 tablespoons lime juice

1 Cook pork, garlic, ginger and spice in a large
non-stick frying pan, stirring, until pork is changed
in colour and cooked through.
2 Add wombok, onion, soy and oyster sauces, and
2 tablespoons of the coriander to pan; cook, stirring,
until wombok is just wilted.

When soaked in hot water, Vietnamese rice-paper sheets (banh trang) make pliable wrappers for a host of fillings. You will need a small wombok (napa cabbage) for this recipe.

3 Place one sheet of rice paper in a medium bowl of warm water until softened slightly; lift sheet carefully from water, place on board, pat dry with absorbent paper. Place one-twelfth of the filling mixture in the centre of the sheet; fold in sides, roll top to bottom to enclose filling. Repeat with remaining rice paper sheets and filling.

4 Combine remaining coriander with the sweet chilli sauce and juice in a small bowl. Serve rolls with sauce mixture.

serving suggestion These pork rolls could be served as a substantial starter before a main course of fried rice or a bowl of chicken broth with rice noodles.

tip Rolls can be prepared a day ahead; store, covered, in the refrigerator.

nutritional count per serving
▶ 7.1g total fat
▶ 2.4g saturated fat
▶ 834kJ (199 cal)
▶ 25.4g carbohydrate
▶ 20.1g protein
▶ 3.7g fibre

Rice stick noodles, also known as sen lek (Thai) and ho fun (Chinese), are wide, flat noodles made from rice flour. Dried noodles must be softened in boiling water before use.

beef and noodle stir-fry

PREP + COOK TIME 35 MINUTES SERVES 4

250g (8 ounces) rice stick noodles

2 teaspoons peanut oil

500g (1 pound) beef eye fillet, sliced thinly

1 tablespoon finely chopped lemon grass

1 clove garlic, crushed

⅓ cup (80ml) lime juice

1 tablespoon fish sauce

100g (3 ounces) baby rocket leaves (arugula)

1 cup (80g) bean sprouts

½ cup loosely packed fresh coriander leaves (cilantro)

½ cup loosely packed fresh mint leaves

3 green onions (scallions), sliced thinly

1 lebanese cucumber (130g), sliced thinly

1 Place noodles in a large heatproof bowl, cover with boiling water; stand 5 minutes or until tender, drain.
2 Heat half the oil in wok; stir-fry beef, in batches, until browned. Remove from wok.
3 Heat remaining oil in wok; stir-fry lemon grass and garlic until fragrant. Return beef to wok with juice and sauce; stir-fry until heated through. Add noodles; stir-fry until combined. Stir in remaining ingredients; serve immediately.

serving suggestion Serve with lime cheeks and a bowl of thinly sliced red thai chilli so diners can adjust the flavours according to their taste.

test kitchen tips

For a more Asian influence, substitute baby tatsoi leaves or chinese water spinach for the rocket. Baby spinach leaves could also be used.

nutritional count per serving
▶ 11.9g total fat
▶ 3.7g saturated fat
▶ 1666kJ (398 cal)
▶ 37.2g carbohydrate
▶ 32.3g protein
▶ 3.7g fibre

Kecap (ketjap) manis is a thick, sweet soy sauce that originated in Indonesia. You need to cook 1 cup (200g) long-grain white rice several hours or a day before making this recipe; spread the cooked still-warm rice on a tray to cool, then cover and refrigerate until required.

fried rice

fried rice

PREP + COOK TIME 20 MINUTES
SERVES 4

cooking-oil spray

2 eggs, beaten lightly

120g (4 ounces) baby corn, halved

1 stalk celery (150g), trimmed, chopped finely

1 small red capsicum (bell pepper) (150g), chopped finely

2 cloves garlic, crushed

140g (4½ ounces) light ham, chopped coarsely

3 cups (450g) cooked long-grain white rice

1 tablespoon kecap manis

4 green onions (scallions), sliced thinly

1 fresh red thai (serrano) chilli, sliced thinly

1 Spray wok with cooking-oil. Pour egg into heated wok; cook over medium heat, tilting pan, until just set. Roll omelette then slice thinly; reserve.
2 Spray heated wok lightly with cooking-oil spray; stir-fry corn and celery for 2 minutes. Add capsicum, garlic and ham; stir-fry 2 minutes. Add rice and kecap manis; stir-fry until heated through. Top rice with omelette, onion and chilli; serve immediately.

serving suggestion Serve with steamed greens or stir-fried vegetables.
tip For information on making the omelette, see page 113.

pea and potato soup

PREP + COOK TIME 40 MINUTES
SERVES 4

3 cups (750ml) chicken stock

2 medium leeks (700g), sliced thinly

1 clove garlic, crushed

2 medium potatoes (400g), chopped coarsely

3 cups (750ml) water

4 cups (480g) frozen peas

2 tablespoons finely shredded fresh mint leaves

1 Heat 2 tablespoons of the stock in a large saucepan, add leek and garlic; cook, stirring, about 10 minutes or until leek is soft.
2 Add remaining stock, potato and the water to the pan; bring to the boil. Reduce heat; simmer, covered, 10 minutes. Add peas, simmer 5 minutes or until vegetables are tender. Cool 10 minutes.
3 Blend or process soup, in batches, until smooth.
4 Return soup to pan; stir over heat until hot. Stir in mint just before serving. Sprinkle with extra mint leaves to serve, if you like.

serving suggestion Herb scones or damper would make a good accompaniment for this soup.
tip For information on washing leeks, see page 112.

photograph page 26

nutritional count per serving
▶ 6.1g total fat
▶ 37g carbohydrate
▶ 1.6g saturated fat
▶ 14.4g protein
▶ 1128kJ (269 cal)
▶ 3.4g fibre

nutritional count per serving
▶ 1.8g total fat
▶ 28.6g carbohydrate
▶ 0.4g saturated fat
▶ 13.4g protein
▶ 869kJ (208 cal)
▶ 11.7g fibre

Leek and potato are natural allies when teamed in a satisfying winter soup. Take care to wash the leeks well under cold water to remove any grit.

pea and potato soup (recipe page 25)

chicken broth with rice noodles (recipe page 28)

test kitchen tips

Coarsely chopped leafy green Chinese vegetables, such as choy sum or water spinach, can be added to this broth. Dried rice noodles, or thicker rice stick noodles, can be substituted for fresh noodles; they need to be soaked in boiling water for about 5 minutes and drained before being added to the stock.

You'll find a version of this popular soup in most Asian cuisines; this one has a Thai accent.

chicken broth with rice noodles

PREP + COOK TIME 40 MINUTES
SERVES 4

1.5 litres (6 cups) chicken stock

2 cups (500ml) water

10cm (4-inch) piece fresh ginger (50g), sliced thinly

350g (11 ounces) chicken breast fillets

500g (1 pound) fresh rice noodles

¼ cup (60ml) lime juice

1 tablespoon fish sauce

4 green onions (scallions), chopped coarsely

2 fresh small red thai (serrano), chillies, seeded, sliced thinly

2 tablespoons coarsely chopped fresh coriander leaves (cilantro)

1 cup (80g) bean sprouts

1 Bring stock, the water and ginger to the boil in a large saucepan. Add chicken, return to the boil, reduce heat; simmer, covered, about 15 minutes or until chicken is cooked through. Remove chicken; cool 10 minutes then shred coarsely. Reserve broth.
2 Return broth mixture to the boil; add noodles, juice and sauce. Reduce heat; simmer, stirring, until noodles are just tender.
3 Add chicken to broth; stir over heat until hot. Divide broth and noodles into serving bowls; sprinkle with remaining ingredients to serve.

photograph page 27

nutritional count per serving
▶ 6.9g total fat
▶ 28.7g carbohydrate
▶ 2.4g saturated fat
▶ 26.4g protein
▶ 1209kJ (289 cal)
▶ 1.9g fibre

penne with tuna and tomato salsa

PREP + COOK TIME 35 MINUTES
SERVES 4

375g (12 ounces) penne

3 medium tomatoes (570g), seeded, chopped finely

1 medium red onion (170g), chopped finely

2 cloves garlic, crushed

¼ cup firmly packed, torn fresh basil leaves

425g (13½ ounces) canned tuna in brine, drained, flaked

¼ cup (60ml) balsamic vinegar

1 Cook pasta in a large saucepan of boiling water, uncovered, until just tender; drain.
2 Combine tomato, onion, garlic, basil, tuna, pasta and vinegar in a large bowl; toss to combine.

serving suggestion Serve with ciabatta bread and a mixed green salad.
tip You can substitute any pasta for the penne in this recipe.

nutritional count per serving
▶ 3.3g total fat
▶ 67.4g carbohydrate
▶ 1g saturated fat
▶ 31.5g protein
▶ 1851kJ (442 cal)
▶ 4.9g fibre

test kitchen tip

The Italian name of this pasta (penne) means 'pen', a reference to the nib-like, pointy ends. Penne comes in both smooth (lisce) or ridged (rigate) versions, and a variety of sizes.

penne with tuna and tomato salsa

A simple covered cooking method replaces the usual labour-intensive non-stop stirring required in more traditional risottos. Best results will be achieved by using arborio rice, but you can use any medium-grain rice, such as calrose.

rice with mushrooms and spinach

PREP + COOK TIME 35 MINUTES **SERVES** 4

3 cups (750ml) vegetable stock

¼ cup (60ml) dry white wine

1 tablespoon finely grated lemon rind

1 medium brown onion (150g), chopped finely

2 cloves garlic, crushed

250g (8 ounces) swiss brown mushrooms, halved

150g (4½ ounces) button mushrooms, halved

1½ cups (300g) arborio rice

2 tablespoons lemon juice

1 cup (250ml) water

100g (3 ounces) baby spinach leaves, torn

½ cup (40g) finely grated parmesan

2 tablespoons fresh baby basil leaves

1 Heat 1 tablespoon of the stock and the wine and lemon rind in a large saucepan; cook onion and garlic, stirring, until onion softens. Add mushrooms; cook, stirring, 5 minutes.
2 Stir in rice, juice, the water and remaining stock. Bring to the boil, reduce heat; simmer, covered, about 20 minutes or until rice is tender.
3 Just before serving, stir in spinach, cheese and basil.

serving suggestion Olive or sourdough bread and a balsamic-dressed mesclun salad turn this dish into a meal.
tip Flat-leaf parsley can be substituted for the basil.

nutritional count per serving
- ▶ 4.9g total fat
- ▶ 2.5g saturated fat
- ▶ 1620kJ (387 cal)
- ▶ 64.4g carbohydrate
- ▶ 15.7g protein
- ▶ 4.6g fibre

steak sandwich

PREP + COOK TIME 30 MINUTES **SERVES** 4

2 small leeks (400g), sliced thinly
1 tablespoon brown sugar
¼ cup (60ml) dry white wine
1 tablespoon wholegrain mustard
2 medium zucchini (240g), sliced thinly
2 baby eggplants (120g), sliced thinly
2 medium tomatoes (300g), sliced thickly
4 x 100g (3 ounces) beef rib-eye steaks
8 slices white bread
50g (1½ ounces) mesclun

1 Cook leek with about 2 tablespoons of water to prevent it sticking, in a medium non-stick frying pan over low heat, stirring, until softened. Add sugar, wine and mustard; cook, stirring, about 10 minutes or until leek is browned and liquid evaporates.

2 Meanwhile, cook zucchini, eggplant and tomato on oiled grill plate (or grill or barbecue) until vegetables are browned all over and just tender. Cover to keep warm.

3 Cook steaks on a heated oiled grill plate (or grill or barbecue) until browned both sides and cooked as desired.

4 Toast bread on a heated oiled grill plate (or grill or barbecue). Sandwich steaks, vegetables and mesclun between toast slices.

serving suggestion Serve with oven-baked potato wedges or thick-cut chips.

tips The leek may be cooked longer to caramelise it, if you prefer. For information on washing leeks, see page 112. Mesclun is a mixture of various baby salad leaves; substitute any single lettuce variety if you prefer. Beef rib-eye is also called scotch fillet by some butchers.

nutritional count per serving
- ▶ 7g total fat
- ▶ 2.3g saturated fat
- ▶ 1458kJ (348 cal)
- ▶ 35.8g carbohydrate
- ▶ 29.3g protein
- ▶ 6.6g fibre

sweet chilli chicken with rice

PREP +COOK TIME 25 MINUTES (+ REFRIGERATION) **SERVES** 4

Garlic, lemon grass and sweet chilli sauce lend a Thai accent to this recipe.

8cm (3¼-inch) piece fresh ginger (40g), grated

3 cloves garlic, crushed

1 tablespoon finely chopped fresh lemon grass

¼ cup (60ml) sweet chilli sauce

¼ cup (60ml) lime juice

½ cup loosely packed, coarsely chopped fresh coriander leaves (cilantro)

4 chicken breast fillets (680g)

¾ cup (150g) long-grain white rice

1 cup (250ml) chicken stock

1 tablespoon cornflour (cornstarch)

1 Combine ginger, garlic, lemon grass, sauce, juice and half the coriander with the chicken in a large bowl, cover; refrigerate 3 hours or overnight.
2 Drain chicken over a large bowl; reserve marinade. Cook chicken, uncovered, in a heated large non-stick frying pan until browned both sides and cooked through; slice chicken thickly.
3 Boil, steam or microwave rice until just tender; drain, then stir in remaining coriander.
4 Meanwhile, blend 2 tablespoons of the stock with cornflour in a small jug. Place remaining stock in a medium saucepan with reserved marinade, bring to the boil. Reduce heat; simmer, stir in cornflour mixture. Cook, stirring, about 5 minutes or until sauce boils and thickens.
5 Serve chicken on rice; drizzle with sauce.

serving suggestion Serve with stir-fried asian greens.
tip Use only the lower white part of the lemon grass stem.

nutritional count per serving	
▶ 10.1g total fat	▶ 44.7g carbohydrate
▶ 3.1g saturated fat	▶ 40.5g protein
▶ 1649kJ (394 cal)	▶ 1.3g fibre

Skim milk keeps the fat count down but the creamy taste intact. You can use any kind of short pasta you like, penne or rigatoni, in place of the shells.

test kitchen tips

Toss the pasta through the sauce just before serving, as it will soak up all the sauce if tossed too early.
Either swiss brown, flat or oyster mushrooms can be used instead of the button mushrooms.

creamy mushroom pasta

creamy mushroom pasta

PREP + COOK TIME 30 MINUTES **SERVES** 4

375g large shell pasta

¼ cup (60ml) vegetable stock

1 clove garlic, crushed

500g (1 pound) button mushrooms, sliced thickly

1 cup (125g) frozen peas

4 green onions (scallions), sliced thinly

1 litre (4 cups) skim milk

2 tablespoons cornflour (cornstarch)

2 tablespoons water

¼ cup coarsely chopped fresh flat-leaf parsley

1 tablespoon wholegrain mustard

½ cup (40g) finely grated parmesan

2 tablespoons finely chopped fresh chives

1 Cook pasta in a large saucepan of boiling water until just tender; drain, keep warm.
2 Bring stock to the boil in the same cleaned saucepan; cook garlic and mushrooms, stirring, until mushrooms soften and liquid evaporates. Stir in peas and half the onion; cook, stirring, until onion softens.
3 Add milk to pan; stir in blended cornflour and the water. Cook, stirring, over low heat until sauce boils and thickens slightly.
4 Remove sauce from heat; stir in pasta, remaining onion, parsley, mustard and cheese. Serve pasta sprinkled with chives. Season to taste.

nutritional count per serving
- ▶ 5.8g total fat
- ▶ 2.7g saturated fat
- ▶ 2285kJ (546 cal)
- ▶ 87.5g carbohydrate
- ▶ 30.9g protein
- ▶ 9g fibre

lamb and pasta salad

PREP + COOK TIME 30 MINUTES **SERVES** 4

400g (12½ ounces) lamb fillets

2 cloves garlic, crushed

1 tablespoon wholegrain mustard

375g (12 ounces) farfalle pasta

250g (8 ounces) yellow teardrop tomatoes, halved

1 medium red onion (170g), sliced thinly

50g (1½ ounces) baby rocket leaves (arugula)

¼ cup loosely packed, finely shredded fresh basil leaves

1 tablespoon fresh thyme leaves

¼ cup (60ml) balsamic vinegar

1 Rub lamb all over with combined garlic and mustard; cook on a heated oiled grill plate (or grill or barbecue) until browned both sides and cooked as desired. Stand 5 minutes, then slice thinly.
2 Meanwhile, cook pasta in a large saucepan of boiling water until just tender; drain.
3 Combine tomato, onion, rocket, basil and thyme in a large bowl.
4 Add pasta, lamb and vinegar to tomato mixture; toss to combine. Season to taste.

photograph page 36

nutritional count per serving
- ▶ 7.2g total fat
- ▶ 2.2g saturated fat
- ▶ 2046kJ (489 cal)
- ▶ 67.8g carbohydrate
- ▶ 33.8g protein
- ▶ 5.3g fibre

test kitchen tips

This salad can be served warm or cold; accompany with some fresh crusty bread. You can substitute your favourite pasta for the farfalle.

lamb and pasta salad (recipe page 35)

tuna and asparagus frittata (recipe page 38)

A frittata, Italian in origin, is a type of omelette cooked in a frying pan, either on the stove top or in the oven, until set. It makes great picnic fare.

tuna and asparagus frittata

PREP + COOK TIME 40 MINUTES **SERVES** 4

4 medium potatoes (800g), sliced thinly

1 medium brown onion (150g), sliced thinly

1 clove garlic, crushed

250g (8 ounces) asparagus, trimmed, chopped coarsely

425g (13½ ounces) canned tuna in spring water, drained

4 eggs, beaten lightly

4 egg whites, beaten lightly

2 tablespoons finely chopped fresh flat-leaf parsley

cooking-oil spray

1 Boil, steam or microwave potato until almost tender.

2 Cook onion and garlic in a heated small non-stick frying pan, stirring, until onion softens.

3 Combine potato and onion mixture in a large bowl with asparagus, tuna, whole egg, egg white and parsley.

4 Preheat grill (broiler). Reheat same frying pan; spray lightly with cooking-oil spray. Spoon frittata mixture into pan, press down firmly; cook, uncovered, over low heat until almost set. Remove from heat; cook under grill until frittata is set and the top is browned lightly. Season to taste.

serving suggestion Serve with a green leafy salad.

photograph page 37

---

nutritional count per serving
- ▶ 8.3g total fat
- ▶ 2.5g saturated fat
- ▶ 1373kJ (328 cal)
- ▶ 24.8g carbohydrate
- ▶ 35.6g protein
- ▶ 4.2g fibre

---

chicken, noodle and mushroom stir-fry

PREP + COOK TIME 30 MINUTES **SERVES** 4

You need about 800g (1½ pounds) of broccoli for this recipe. Hokkien (or stir-fry) noodles are sold in cryovac packages in the refrigerated section of supermarkets.

450g (1 pound) hokkien noodles

500g (1 pound) chicken thigh fillets, chopped coarsely

1 clove garlic, crushed

200g (6½ ounces) broccoli florets

150g (4½ ounces) oyster mushrooms, halved

1 medium red onion (170g), sliced thinly

200g (6½ ounces) snow peas, halved

¼ cup (60ml) oyster sauce

1 fresh red thai (serrano) chilli, sliced thinly

1 Rinse noodles under hot water; drain. Transfer to a large bowl; separate noodles with a fork.

2 Stir-fry chicken in a heated lightly oiled wok, in batches, until browned and cooked through. Remove chicken from wok.

3 Stir-fry garlic, broccoli, mushrooms and onion in wok until onion just softens. Return chicken to wok with noodles, snow peas and sauce; stir-fry until vegetables are just tender. Sprinkle with chilli; season to taste.

tip Snow peas can be replaced with sugar snap peas, if you like.

---

nutritional count per serving
- ▶ 12.3g total fat
- ▶ 3.4g saturated fat
- ▶ 2316kJ (553 cal)
- ▶ 67g carbohydrate
- ▶ 38.5g protein
- ▶ 7.8g fibre

chicken, noodle and mushroom stir-fry

moroccan lamb with couscous

PREP + COOK TIME 30 MINUTES (+ REFRIGERATION) SERVES 4

8 lamb fillets (700g)

1 tablespoon ground cumin

1 tablespoon ground coriander

1 teaspoon ground cinnamon

¾ cup (210g) low-fat yoghurt

1½ cups (300g) couscous

1½ cups (375ml) boiling water

1 teaspoon peanut oil

⅓ cup (55g) dried currants

2 teaspoons finely grated lemon rind

2 teaspoons lemon juice

¼ cup firmly packed fresh coriander leaves (cilantro)

1 Combine lamb, spices and ⅓ cup of the yoghurt in a medium bowl, cover; refrigerate for 3 hours or overnight.

2 Cook lamb on a heated oiled grill plate (or grill or barbecue) until browned and cooked as desired. Cover; stand 5 minutes, then slice thinly.

3 Meanwhile, combine couscous, the water and oil in a large heatproof bowl, cover; stand 5 minutes or until liquid is absorbed, fluffing with a fork occasionally. Stir currants, rind, juice and fresh coriander into couscous; toss with a fork to combine.

4 Drizzle lamb with remaining yoghurt to serve; accompany with couscous.

test kitchen tips

You could substitute some finely chopped preserved lemon rind for the lemon rind in the couscous. Accompany with harissa, the fiery North African condiment, for added heat.

nutritional count per serving
- ▶ 13.9g total fat
- ▶ 4.4g saturated fat
- ▶ 2640kJ (631 cal)
- ▶ 72.3g carbohydrate
- ▶ 51.2g protein
- ▶ 2.4g fibre

test kitchen tips

Lightly oil the tablespoon
to make the honey easier
to measure.
You can grill or barbecue
the chicken rather than
bake it.

honey-mustard chicken with potato kumara mash

PREP + COOK TIME 30 MINUTES (+ REFRIGERATION) **SERVES** 4

Soak eight bamboo skewers in water for at least 30 minutes before using to prevent them from scorching during cooking.

8 chicken tenderloins (600g)

⅓ cup (115g) honey

2 tablespoons wholegrain mustard

⅓ cup (80ml) white vinegar

2 tablespoons soy sauce

3 medium potatoes (600g)

1 small kumara (orange sweet potato) (250g)

2 cloves garlic, sliced thinly

¼ cup (60ml) skim milk

2 teaspoons fresh thyme leaves

1 Thread each piece of chicken onto a bamboo skewer; place in a shallow baking dish. Pour half of the combined honey, mustard, vinegar and sauce over chicken, cover; refrigerate 3 hours or overnight.

2 Preheat oven to 220°C/425°F.

3 Roast undrained chicken, uncovered, about 10 minutes or until cooked through.

4 Meanwhile, coarsely chop potatoes and kumara. Boil, steam or microwave combined potato, kumara and garlic until tender; drain. Mash in a medium bowl with milk, stir in thyme; season to taste.

5 Bring the remaining marinade to the boil in a small saucepan.

6 Serve chicken with potato kumara mash; drizzle with marinade, sprinkle with extra fresh thyme leaves before serving, if you like.

serving suggestion Serve with steamed green vegetables or a green salad.

nutritional count per serving
▶ 8.8g total fat
▶ 2.6g saturated fat
▶ 1830kJ (437 cal)
▶ 49.2g carbohydrate
▶ 38g protein
▶ 3.6g fibre

nutritional count per serving
- ▶ 17.8g total fat
- ▶ 9.4g saturated fat
- ▶ 1493kJ (357 cal)
- ▶ 22.2g carbohydrate
- ▶ 23.9g protein
- ▶ 5g fibre

salmon and roast potato salad

PREP + COOK TIME 40 MINUTES (+ COOLING) **SERVES** 4

500g kipfler (fingerling) potatoes, unpeeled, chopped coarsely

415g (13 ounces) canned pink salmon

2 medium tomatoes (300g), sliced thickly

1 baby cos lettuce, torn roughly

½ cup (120g) sour cream

1 small red onion (100g), chopped finely

¼ cup (50g) rinsed, drained capers, chopped finely

2 tablespoons finely chopped fresh dill

2 tablespoons lemon juice

1 Preheat oven to 220°C/425°F.

2 Place potato in a large lightly oiled baking dish; roast, uncovered, stirring occasionally, about 30 minutes or until browned and crisp. Allow potato to cool.

3 Drain salmon, discard any bones and skin; flake with a fork into a large serving bowl.

4 Place cooled potato in bowl with salmon; add tomato and lettuce, toss to combine.

5 Drizzle salad with combined remaining ingredients just before serving; season to taste.

rosemary lamb open sandwich

PREP + COOK TIME 20 MINUTES (+ REFRIGERATION) **SERVES** 4

4 lamb fillets (320g)

2 cloves garlic, crushed

¼ cup (60ml) lemon juice

2 tablespoons fresh rosemary leaves

1 tablespoon wholegrain mustard

200g (6½ ounces) mixed cherry tomatoes

250g (8 ounces) asparagus, trimmed, halved

4 slices light rye bread

8 small butter lettuce leaves

1 Combine lamb, garlic, juice, rosemary and mustard in a small bowl, cover; refrigerate 3 hours or overnight.

2 Cook tomato and asparagus, in batches, on a heated oiled grill plate (or grill or barbecue) until browned lightly and just tender.

3 Drain lamb; discard marinade. Cook lamb on the same heated grill plate (or grill or barbecue) until browned and cooked as desired. Cover; stand 5 minutes before slicing thickly.

4 Meanwhile, toast bread on the heated grill plate (or grill or barbecue) both sides. Place one slice of toast on each serving plate; top each with lettuce, tomato, asparagus and lamb. Season.

serving suggestion Dollop a spoonful of guacamole or low-fat mayonnaise, flavoured with crushed garlic, on each sandwich.
tip You can substitute toasted sourdough or ciabatta for the rye bread.

nutritional count per serving
▶ 6.5g total fat
▶ 1.8g saturated fat
▶ 1038kJ (248 cal)
▶ 21g carbohydrate
▶ 23.2g protein
▶ 4.9g fibre

greek barbecued prawn salad

PREP + COOK TIME 20 MINUTES **SERVES** 4

Capture the essence of an Aegean summer with this flavour-packed Greek-style salad.

⅓ cup (80ml) lemon juice

1 tablespoon honey

4 cloves garlic, crushed

¼ teaspoon cayenne pepper

600g (1¼ pounds) peeled green prawns, tails intact

¼ cup (60ml) lemon juice, extra

1½ tablespoons honey, extra

100g (3 ounces) baby spinach leaves

1 small red onion (100g) sliced thinly

250g (8 ounces) cherry tomatoes, halved

1 tablespoon finely shredded fresh mint leaves

1 tablespoon finely shredded fresh basil leaves

100g (3 ounces) fetta, chopped coarsely

1 Combine the juice, honey, garlic, pepper and prawns in a large bowl.
2 Cook prawns, on a heated oiled grill plate (or barbecue or grill) until browned and just cooked through.
3 Meanwhile, combine extra juice and honey in a small jug.
4 Combine prawns with remaining ingredients in a large bowl; drizzle with dressing, toss to combine. Season to taste.

serving suggestion Serve with a bowl of tzatziki, that piquant Greek combination of cucumber, yoghurt and garlic.

nutritional count per serving
▶ 7.1g total fat
▶ 4.2g saturated fat
▶ 1184kJ (283 cal)
▶ 15.5g carbohydrate
▶ 37g protein
▶ 2.7g fibre

test kitchen tip

You could substitute rocket or any other salad green for the spinach.

test kitchen tip

Fish can be coated in
the crumb mixture up to
2 hours before cooking
time; store, covered,
in the refrigerator.

crumbed fish with warm tomato salad

PREP + COOK TIME 40 MINUTES **SERVES** 4

You can use flathead, snapper, ling, bream or any other firm white fish in this recipe.

cooking-oil spray

1 medium red onion (170g), cut into thin wedges

250g (8 ounces) heirloom tomato mix

¼ cup (60ml) white wine vinegar

2 cloves garlic, crushed

½ cup (80g) corn flake crumbs

1 teaspoon each of ground cumin, turmeric and sweet paprika

4 firm white fish fillets (720g)

¼ cup (35g) plain (all-purpose) flour

2 egg whites, beaten lightly

150g baby spinach leaves

¼ cup (50g) rinsed, drained capers

1 Preheat oven to 220°C/425°F.

2 Spray oven tray lightly with cooking-oil spray. Place onion and tomatoes on tray; drizzle with combined vinegar and garlic. Roast, uncovered, about 20 minutes or until tomatoes are softened.

3 Combine crumbs and spices in a small bowl. Coat fish in flour; shake away excess. Dip fish in egg white, then coat in crumb mixture. Spray fish, both sides, with cooking-oil spray; cook, uncovered, in a heated large non-stick frying pan until browned both sides and cooked through.

4 Combine spinach and capers in a large bowl with tomato and onion mixture; serve with fish, season.

serving suggestion Serve with yoghurt combined with capers and chopped fresh flat-leaf parsley.

---

nutritional count per serving
- ▶ 6.3g total fat
- ▶ 1.4g saturated fat
- ▶ 1471kJ (351 cal)
- ▶ 29.4g carbohydrate
- ▶ 42.2g protein
- ▶ 4.1g fibre

MAINS

satay beef stir-fry with hokkien noodles

PREP + COOK TIME 30 MINUTES SERVES 4

Kecap (ketjap) manis, a thick sweet soy sauce of Indonesian origin, is available at many supermarkets and Asian food stores.

600g (1¼ pounds) hokkien noodles

300g (9½ ounces) beef rump steak, sliced thinly

1cm (½-inch) piece fresh ginger (5g) grated finely

2 teaspoons sesame oil

1 small red onion (100g), sliced thinly

1 medium red capsicum (bell pepper) (200g), sliced thinly

150g (4½ ounces) broccoli florets

2 teaspoons lime juice

¼ cup (75g) satay sauce

1 tablespoon hoisin sauce

⅓ cup (80ml) soy sauce

1 tablespoon kecap manis

150g (4½ ounces) snow peas

1 tablespoon finely chopped fresh coriander leaves (cilantro)

¼ cup (35g) unsalted roasted peanuts, chopped coarsely

1 Place noodles in a large heatproof bowl, cover with boiling water; separate with a fork, drain.
2 Heat oiled wok; stir-fry beef and ginger, in batches, until browned. Remove from wok.
3 Heat oil in same wok; stir-fry onion, capsicum and broccoli until just tender. Return beef to wok with combined juice and sauces; stir-fry until sauce boils. Add noodles and snow peas; stir-fry until hot.
4 Add coriander; stir-fry until combined. Sprinkle with peanuts, and extra coriander leaves, if you like, before serving.

serving suggestion Accompany with a bowl of sambal oelek, the fiery-hot Indonesian chilli and vinegar sauce.
tip You can substitute your favourite noodles in place of hokkien noodles.

These grills, bakes, pastas, curries and stir-fries come complete with accompaniments, for ease of planning and preparation, and for keeping track of fat and kilojoule counts.

nutritional count per serving
- ▶ 16.8g total fat
- ▶ 4.2g saturated fat
- ▶ 2887kJ (690 cal)
- ▶ 90.8g carbohydrate
- ▶ 38.9g protein
- ▶ 7.9g fibre

mustard veal with polenta and spinach puree

PREP + COOK TIME 35 MINUTES SERVES 4

⅓ cup (95g) wholegrain mustard

2 tablespoons coarsely chopped fresh oregano

4 cloves garlic

4 veal chops (800g)

4 large egg (plum) tomatoes (360g), halved

2 cups (500ml) water

1 teaspoon salt

1 cup (170g) polenta

¾ cup (180ml) skim milk

¼ cup (20g) finely grated parmesan

2kg (4 pounds) spinach, trimmed

2 anchovy fillets, drained

2 tablespoons lemon juice

¼ cup (60ml) beef stock

1 Preheat grill (broiler) to medium high. Combine mustard, oregano and 2 crushed garlic cloves in a small bowl; brush veal both sides with mustard mixture. Cook veal under grill until browned both sides and cooked as desired.

2 Cook tomato, in batches, on heated lightly oiled grill plate (or grill or barbecue) until tender.

3 Meanwhile, bring combined water and salt to the boil in a medium saucepan. Stir in polenta; cook, stirring, about 10 minutes or until polenta thickens. Stir in milk; cook, stirring, about 5 minutes or until polenta thickens. Stir in cheese.

Polenta is the Italian answer to mashed potato – it's the perfect accompaniment for soaking up meat juices and too-good-to-waste sauces.

4 Boil, steam or microwave spinach until just wilted. When cool enough to handle, squeeze out excess liquid with hands. Crush remaining garlic. Blend or process spinach with garlic and remaining ingredients until pureed.

5 Serve veal with tomato, polenta and spinach mixture; sprinkle with extra oregano leaves before serving, if you like.

serving suggestion Top steaks with fresh sage leaves, and serve with radicchio or rocket salad dressed with balsamic vinegar.
tips Lower the shelf of the grill to cook the veal. Fresh rosemary or thyme can be substituted for the oregano.

nutritional count per serving
▶ 8.2g total fat
▶ 2.7g saturated fat
▶ 1805kJ (431 cal)
▶ 37.1g carbohydrate
▶ 45.3g protein
▶ 11.1g fibre

pork fillet with apple and leek

PREP + COOK TIME 35 MINUTES **SERVES** 4

Pork has a natural affinity with both apple and onion; here, these traditional accompaniments are given a contemporary twist.

800g (1½ pounds) pork fillets

¾ cup (180ml) chicken stock

2 medium leeks (700g), sliced thickly

1 clove garlic, crushed

2 tablespoons brown sugar

2 tablespoons red wine vinegar

10g (½ ounce) butter

2 medium apples (300g), unpeeled, sliced thinly

1 tablespoon brown sugar, extra

400g (12½ ounces) baby carrots, trimmed

8 medium patty-pan squash (240g), quartered

250g (8 ounces) asparagus, trimmed, chopped coarsely

1 Preheat oven to 240°C/475°F.

2 Cook pork in heated oiled frying pan, over medium-high heat, until browned all over. Place, in a single layer, in a large baking dish; bake, uncovered, in oven, about 20 minutes or until pork is cooked as desired. Cover; stand 5 minutes before slicing thickly.

3 Meanwhile, heat half the stock in a medium frying pan; cook leek and garlic, stirring, until leek softens and browns slightly. Add sugar and vinegar; cook, stirring, about 5 minutes or until leek caramelises. Add remaining stock; bring to the boil. Reduce heat; simmer, uncovered, about 5 minutes or until liquid reduces by half. Place leek mixture in a medium bowl; cover to keep warm.

4 Melt butter in same pan; cook apple and extra sugar, stirring, until apple is browned and tender.

5 Boil, steam or microwave carrot, squash and asparagus, separately, until just tender; drain.

6 Divide carrot, squash and asparagus among serving plates; top with pork and caramelised apple and leek, season.

serving suggestion Potatoes – boiled, mashed or baked – would make a good accompaniment for this dish.

nutritional count per serving
- ▶ 9.6g total fat
- ▶ 4.3g saturated fat
- ▶ 1690kJ (404 cal)
- ▶ 25.2g carbohydrate
- ▶ 50g protein
- ▶ 8.9g fibre

test kitchen tips

You can make the sweet
and sour leek several
hours ahead; reheat just
before serving. For
information on washing
leeks and crushing garlic,
see page 112.

Contrasting colours add appeal to this fragrant curry, which is traditionally served with flatbreads, such as naan or puri, in Indian homes. You can substitute equivalent weights of peas, capsicum, mushrooms or zucchini if you prefer them to the vegetables suggested.

cauliflower, potato and bean curry

serving suggestion
Accompany with pappadums, and raita made with low-fat yoghurt and cucumber.

cauliflower, potato and bean curry

PREP + COOK TIME 30 MINUTES **SERVES** 4

4 eggs

1 medium brown onion (150g), sliced thickly

2 fresh small red thai (serrano) chillies, chopped coarsely

1 clove garlic, crushed

2 tablespoons mild curry paste

500g (1 pound) cauliflower florets

4 small potatoes (480g), chopped coarsely

1½ cups (375ml) vegetable stock

1½ cups (375ml) water

2 cups (400g) jasmine rice

200g (6½ ounces) green beans, halved

400ml (12½ ounces) light coconut milk

¼ cup loosely packed fresh coriander leaves (cilantro)

1 Boil eggs in a large saucepan of water about 6 minutes or until hard; cool, then peel and halve.
2 Cook onion, chilli and garlic in a heated large non-stick saucepan, stirring, until onion softens. Stir in paste until fragrant. Add cauliflower and potato; cook, stirring, until coated in curry mixture. Add stock and the water; bring to the boil, then simmer, covered, until potato is just tender.
3 Meanwhile, cook rice in a large saucepan of boiling water, uncovered, until just tender; drain. Cover to keep warm.
4 Stir beans into curry mixture; cook, uncovered, until just tender. Stir in coconut milk and egg; simmer, uncovered, until hot. Serve curry with rice; sprinkle with coriander.

nutritional count per serving
▸ 17.9g total fat   ▸ 103.7g carbohydrate
▸ 8.9g saturated fat   ▸ 23.1g protein
▸ 2892kJ (691 cal)   ▸ 8.7g fibre

pork with ratatouille and potatoes

PREP + COOK TIME 35 MINUTES **SERVES** 4

1kg (2 pounds) baby new (chat) potatoes, quartered

1 medium brown onion (150g), chopped coarsely

2 cloves garlic, crushed

4 baby eggplants (240g), sliced thickly

2 medium zucchini (240g), sliced thickly

400g (12½ ounces) canned crushed tomatoes

2 tablespoons finely shredded fresh basil leaves

4 x 150g (4½ ounces) pork steaks (medallions)

1 Preheat oven to 240°C/475°F.
2 Place potato in a large lightly oiled baking dish; roast, uncovered, about 25 minutes or until potato is browned and crisp.
3 Meanwhile, cook onion and garlic in a heated large non-stick frying pan, stirring, until onion softens. Add eggplant and zucchini; cook, stirring, until vegetables are just tender.
4 Stir tomatoes into pan; bring to the boil. Reduce heat; simmer, uncovered, about 5 minutes or until vegetables are tender and sauce thickens. Stir in basil. Season to taste.
5 Cook pork, in batches, in a heated medium non-stick frying pan until browned both sides and cooked as desired.
6 Serve pork with potatoes and ratatouille.

serving suggestion A green salad goes well with this dish.

photograph page 58

nutritional count per serving
▸ 4.2g total fat   ▸ 40.3g carbohydrate
▸ 1.1g saturated fat   ▸ 43.7g protein
▸ 1672kJ (399 cal)   ▸ 9.5g fibre

test kitchen tip

Ratatouille can be made a day ahead; store, covered, in the refrigerator. It is great on its own, or served with pasta.

In a Provençale dialect, touiller means to stir and crush, thus the name ratatouille perfectly describes this rich vegetable stew.

pork with ratatouille and potatoes (recipe page 57)

chickpea and pumpkin curry (recipe page 60)

test kitchen tip

Make the curry a day ahead to allow the flavours to develop.

In Indian cooking, the word masala loosely translates as 'paste'; the word tikka refers to a bite-sized piece of meat, poultry, fish or vegetable. A jar labelled tikka masala contains spices and oils, blended into a mild paste.

chickpea and pumpkin curry

PREP + COOK TIME 35 MINUTES **SERVES** 4

2 teaspoons peanut oil

2 medium brown onions (300g), sliced thinly

2 cloves garlic, crushed

2 tablespoons tikka masala curry paste

2 cups (500ml) vegetable stock

1 cup (250ml) water

1kg (2 pounds) butternut pumpkin, chopped coarsely

2 cups (400g) jasmine rice

300g (9½ ounces) canned chickpeas (garbanzo beans), rinsed, drained

1 cup (125g) frozen peas

¼ cup (60ml) light thickened (heavy) cream

⅓ cup fresh coriander leaves (cilantro)

1 Heat oil in a large saucepan; cook onion and garlic, stirring, until onion softens. Add paste; cook, stirring, until fragrant. Stir in stock and the water; bring to the boil. Add pumpkin; reduce heat. Simmer, covered, 15 minutes or until pumpkin is almost tender.

2 Meanwhile, cook rice in a large saucepan of boiling water until tender; drain. Cover to keep warm.

3 Add chickpeas and peas to curry; cook, stirring, until hot. Stir in cream and top with coriander. Serve curry with rice.

serving suggestion Accompany with a fresh tomato sambal, pickles or chutney, and pappadums.

photograph page 59

nutritional count per serving	
▶ 10.4g total fat	▶ 110.1g carbohydrate
▶ 4g saturated fat	▶ 19.1g protein
▶ 2648kJ (633 cal)	▶ 9.8g fibre

gnocchi with herb and mushroom sauce

PREP + COOK TIME 25 MINUTES **SERVES** 4

1 tablespoon vegetable oil

1 medium brown onion (150g), chopped coarsely

2 cloves garlic, crushed

400g (12½ ounces) swiss brown mushrooms, sliced thinly

1 tablespoon plain (all-purpose) flour

⅓ cup (80ml) dry red wine

2 teaspoons soy sauce

⅔ cup (160ml) vegetable stock

1 tablespoon light sour cream

1 tablespoon coarsely chopped fresh oregano

1 tablespoon finely chopped fresh sage

600g (1¼ pounds) fresh potato gnocchi

1 Heat oil in a large frying pan; cook onion, garlic and mushrooms, stirring, until vegetables are just tender. Add flour; cook, stirring, 1 minute.

2 Add wine, sauce, stock and cream; cook, stirring, until sauce thickens slightly. Stir in herbs.

3 Meanwhile, cook gnocchi in a large saucepan of boiling water until gnocchi rise to the surface and are just tender; drain. Add gnocchi to herb and mushroom sauce; toss gently to combine.

serving suggestion A green salad, dressed with herb vinaigrette, and fresh crusty bread.
tip You could substitute button or oyster mushrooms for the swiss browns.

nutritional count per serving	
▶ 7.5g total fat	▶ 49.8g carbohydrate
▶ 1.9g saturated fat	▶ 11.6g protein
▶ 1438kJ (343 cal)	▶ 6.9g fibre

Gnocchi are small dumplings made of such ingredients as flour, potatoes, semolina, ricotta cheese or spinach. They make a great base for a full-flavoured sauce, such as this, packed with herbs, red wine and mushrooms.

gnocchi with herb and mushroom sauce

Croûton comes from the French word croûte, which translates as crust – hence these crunchy pieces of garlic bread soak up the sauce in this dish.

warm lamb salad with croûtons

PREP + COOK TIME 25 MINUTES **SERVES** 4

4 slices white bread (180g)

1 tablespoon vegetable oil

1 clove garlic, crushed

4 medium zucchini (480g), sliced thinly

4 baby eggplants (240g), sliced thinly

8 french-trimmed lamb cutlets (400g)

½ cup (125ml) balsamic vinegar

½ cup (125ml) beef stock

75g (2½ ounces) curly endive

3 medium tomatoes (450g), chopped coarsely

1 Preheat oven to 220°C/425°F.

2 Discard crusts from bread. Halve each slice diagonally. Combine oil and garlic in a small bowl; add bread, toss to coat in oil mixture. Place bread, in a single layer, on oven tray; toast in oven, turning once, for about 4 minutes each side or until croûtons are browned lightly and crisp.

3 Cook zucchini and eggplant, in batches, in a heated large non-stick frying pan until just tender; remove from pan, cover to keep warm.

4 Cook lamb, in batches, in the same pan until browned both sides and cooked as desired; remove from pan, cover to keep warm.

5 Place vinegar in same pan; bring to the boil. Add stock; reduce heat. Simmer, uncovered, until sauce reduces by half.

6 Serve lamb on croûtons with combined zucchini, eggplant, endive and tomato. Drizzle with balsamic dressing, if you like.

tip Croûtons can be made a day ahead and stored in an airtight container.

nutritional count per serving
▶ 10.4g total fat
▶ 2.5g saturated fat
▶ 937kJ (223 cal)
▶ 13.1g carbohydrate
▶ 15.4g protein
▶ 5.7g fibre

lamb chermoulla with chickpea salad

PREP + COOK TIME 30 MINUTES SERVES 4

300g (9½ ounces) green beans, trimmed

2 teaspoons each cracked black pepper, and ground cumin and coriander

1 teaspoon hot paprika

2 tablespoons each coarsely chopped fresh mint, flat-leaf parsley and coriander (cilantro)

1 tablespoon coarsely grated lemon rind

¼ cup (60ml) water

1 medium red onion (170g), chopped finely

8 lamb fillets (700g)

400g (12½ ounces) canned brown lentils, rinsed, drained

300g (9½ ounces) canned chickpeas (garbanzo beans), rinsed, drained

⅓ cup loosely packed, torn fresh flat-leaf parsley, extra

2 cloves garlic, crushed

2 tablespoons lemon juice

1 Cut beans into 3cm lengths; boil, steam or microwave until just tender. Refresh under cold water; drain.

2 To make chermoulla paste, blend or process spices, herbs, rind, the water and half the onion until mixture forms a paste.

3 Coat lamb with chermoulla paste in a large bowl; cook, in batches, on a heated oiled grill plate (or grill or barbecue) until browned and cooked as desired. Cover; stand 5 minutes before slicing thickly.

4 Combine beans, lentils, chickpeas, extra parsley, garlic and juice with remaining onion in a large bowl; toss gently to combine. Serve salad with lamb.

serving suggestion Accompany with a bowl of minted yoghurt.

nutritional count per serving
▶ 14.2g total fat
▶ 5.8g saturated fat
▶ 1664kJ (398 cal)
▶ 17.1g carbohydrate
▶ 45.9g protein
▶ 7.9g fibre

Chermoulla is a Moroccan blend of herbs and spices, including coriander, cumin and paprika, traditionally used for preserving or seasoning chicken, meat and fish.

test kitchen tip

The salad can be assembled several hours ahead; add juice just before serving.

test kitchen tip

Mash can be made a day ahead; store, covered, in the refrigerator. Reheat just before serving.

steak bourguignon with celeriac potato mash

PREP + COOK TIME 30 MINUTES **SERVES** 4

You can substitute rib-eye (scotch fillet) or sirloin (new-york cut) steak for the eye fillet in this recipe.

1 small celeriac (400g), chopped coarsely

2 medium potatoes (400g), chopped coarsely

¼ cup (60ml) skim milk

20g (¾ ounce) butter

4 x 200g (6½ ounces) beef eye-fillet steaks

200g (6½ ounces) button mushrooms, halved

6 baby onions (150g), quartered

2 cloves garlic, crushed

½ cup (125ml) dry red wine

1 cup (250ml) beef stock

1 tablespoon tomato paste

2 teaspoons cornflour (cornstarch)

2 teaspoons water

1 tablespoon coarsely chopped fresh oregano

1 Boil, steam or microwave celeriac and potato, separately, until tender; drain. Mash in a medium bowl with milk and butter; cover to keep warm.

2 Meanwhile, cook beef in a heated large non-stick frying pan until browned both sides and cooked as desired; cover to keep warm.

3 Cook mushrooms, onion and garlic in same pan until vegetables just soften. Add wine, stock and paste; simmer, uncovered, about 5 minutes. Stir in blended cornflour and the water; cook, stirring, until sauce boils and thickens.

4 Serve beef with mash and bourguignon sauce; sprinkle with oregano.

serving suggestion Steamed greens such as asparagus or broccoli.

---

nutritional count per serving
▶ 17.2g total fat
▶ 7.6g saturated fat
▶ 1962kJ (469 cal)
▶ 20.1g carbohydrate
▶ 49.5g protein
▶ 6.4g fibre

pad thai

PREP + COOK TIME 15 MINUTES **SERVES** 4

250g dried rice stick noodles

450g chicken thigh fillets, sliced thinly

1 clove garlic, crushed

1cm (½-inch) piece fresh ginger (5g), grated

2 fresh small red thai (serrano) chillies, sliced thinly

2 tablespoons grated palm sugar

2 tablespoons soy sauce

¼ cup (60ml) sweet chilli sauce

1 tablespoon fish sauce

1 tablespoon lime juice

3 green onions (scallions), sliced thinly

1 cup (80g) bean sprouts

1 cup (80g) snow pea sprouts

¼ cup loosely packed fresh coriander leaves (cilantro)

1 Place noodles in a large heatproof bowl; cover with boiling water. Stand until just tender; drain.

2 Heat lightly oiled wok; stir-fry chicken, garlic, ginger and chilli, in batches, until chicken is browned all over.

3 Return chicken mixture to wok with sugar, sauces and juice; stir-fry until sauce thickens slightly. Add noodles, onion and half of the sprouts to wok; stir-fry until hot. Sprinkle with coriander and remaining sprouts to serve. Season; accompany with lime cheeks, if you like.

serving suggestion Although this dish is a complete meal in a bowl, the Thais usually accompany it with a soup such as tom yum goong (prawn soup), which is consumed like a beverage throughout the meal.

nutritional count per serving
▶ 10.3g total fat
▶ 2.8g saturated fat
▶ 1578kJ (377 cal)
▶ 55g carbohydrate
▶ 25g protein
▶ 2.2g fibre

Noodles are a favourite Thai snack, and for this dish, sen lek, a 5mm (¼-inch) wide rice stick noodle, is used.

test kitchen tips

Remove membranes and seeds from the chillies if you prefer less heat. Palm sugar, also sold as jaggery, is a product of the coconut palm. It usually comes in hard blocks; substitute brown sugar if you can't find it at your supermarket. For information on grating palm sugar, see page 112.

test kitchen tips

You can make the capsicum
relish a day ahead; store,
covered, in the refrigerator.
Reheat just before serving.
See page 112 for information
on removing kernels from
corn cobs.

beef steak with capsicum relish

PREP + COOK TIME 30 MINUTES **SERVES** 4

You can substitute rib-eye (scotch fillet) or sirloin (new-york cut) steak for the eye fillet in this recipe.

3 medium red capsicums (bell peppers) (600g)

1 teaspoon olive oil

1 large brown onion (200g), sliced thinly

2 cloves garlic, sliced thinly

2 tablespoons brown sugar

2 tablespoons sherry vinegar

3 fresh small red thai (serrano) chillies, seeded, chopped finely

4 x 200g (6½ ounces) beef eye fillet steaks

2 corn cobs (800g), trimmed, chopped coarsely

150g (4½ ounces) sugar snap peas

300g (9½ ounces) baby new (chat) potatoes

2 tablespoons coarsely chopped fresh flat-leaf parsley

1 Preheat grill (broiler).

2 Quarter capsicums; discard seeds and membranes. Roast under grill, skin-side up, until skin blisters and blackens. Cover with plastic or paper for 5 minutes, then peel away skin (see page 112); slice thinly.

3 Heat oil in a medium frying pan; cook onion and garlic, stirring, until soft. Add sugar, vinegar, chilli and capsicum; cook, stirring, 5 minutes.

4 Meanwhile, cook beef on a heated oiled grill plate (or grill or barbecue) until browned and cooked as desired.

5 Boil, steam or microwave corn, peas and potatoes, separately, until just tender; drain.

6 Top steaks with capsicum relish; serve with vegetables, sprinkle with parsley.

serving suggestion A green salad.

nutritional count per serving
▶ 11.2g total fat
▶ 4.4g saturated fat
▶ 1714kJ (409 cal)
▶ 25.9g carbohydrate
▶ 47.7g protein
▶ 4.5g fibre

tandoori lamb with cucumber raita

PREP + COOK TIME 30 MINUTES **SERVES** 4

½ teaspoon ground cumin

1 teaspoon ground cardamom

8 lamb fillets (700g)

1 tablespoon tandoori paste

2 x 200g (12½-ounce) tubs low-fat yoghurt

1 lebanese cucumber (130g), seeded, chopped finely

2 green onions (scallions), chopped finely

2 cups (400g) basmati rice

pinch saffron threads

1 Combine ground cumin and cardamom.

2 Combine lamb with paste and half the yoghurt in a large bowl. Combine remaining yoghurt in a small bowl with cucumber, onion and half of the combined spices.

3 Place rice and saffron in a large saucepan of boiling water; cook until rice is tender. Drain; place rice in a large bowl.

4 Toast remaining spices in a heated dry small frying pan until fragrant; stir into saffron rice, cover to keep warm.

5 Cook undrained lamb, in batches, on a heated lightly oiled grill plate (or grill or barbecue) until browned and cooked as desired.

6 Serve lamb on saffron rice, accompany with cucumber raita.

serving suggestion A fresh tomato and onion sambal, and pappadums.

tips You can marinate the lamb a day ahead; store, covered, in the refrigerator. The cucumber raita can be made several hours ahead; store, covered, in the refrigerator.

nutritional count per serving
- 13.1g total fat
- 5.8g saturated fat
- 2822kJ (674 cal)
- 86.9g carbohydrate
- 49.5g protein
- 1.5g fibre

chicken and potato casserole

PREP + COOK TIME 45 MINUTES **SERVES** 4

1 tablespoon peanut oil

6 baby onions (150g), quartered

2 cloves garlic, crushed

700g (1½ ounces) chicken thigh fillets, chopped coarsely

300g (9½ ounces) baby new (chat) potatoes, quartered

1 large carrot (180g), chopped coarsely

¼ cup (35g) plain (all-purpose) flour

⅓ cup (80ml) dry white wine

420g (13½ ounces) canned chicken consommé

250g (8 ounces) asparagus, trimmed, cut into 5cm (2-inch) pieces

2 tablespoons wholegrain mustard

1 tablespoon finely grated lemon rind

⅓ cup loosely packed, coarsely chopped fresh flat-leaf parsley

1 Heat oil in a large non-stick saucepan; cook onion and garlic, stirring, until onion softens. Add chicken; cook, stirring, about 5 minutes or until chicken is browned and cooked through.

2 Add potato, carrot and flour to pan; cook, stirring, 5 minutes. Add wine and consommé; cook, stirring, until mixture boils and thickens. Simmer, covered, about 10 minutes or until potato is tender.

3 Add asparagus, mustard and rind to pan; bring to the boil. Reduce heat; simmer, covered, until asparagus is just tender. Stir in rind and parsley.

serving suggestion A radicchio, coral and oakleaf lettuce salad.

tip This recipe is more flavoursome if made a day ahead; store, covered, in the refrigerator. Reheat just before serving.

nutritional count per serving

▶ 21.4g total fat   ▶ 24.5g carbohydrate
▶ 5.7g saturated fat   ▶ 36.7g protein
▶ 1934kJ (462 cal)   ▶ 6g fibre

The spices of North Africa give the chicken a flavour-packed jolt in this dish. And, as it can be served hot or cold, this recipe is a good prepare-ahead dish.

chicken with lentil salsa

PREP + COOK TIME 25 MINUTES SERVES 4

2 teaspoons each ground cumin and ground coriander

1 teaspoon ground turmeric

12 chicken tenderloins (900g)

1½ cups (300g) dried red lentils

1 clove garlic, crushed

1 fresh small red thai (serrano) chilli, seeded, chopped finely

1 lebanese cucumber (130g), seeded, chopped finely

1 medium red capsicum (bell pepper) (200g), chopped finely

¼ cup (60ml) lemon juice

2 teaspoons peanut oil

2 tablespoons coarsely chopped fresh coriander leaves (cilantro)

2 limes, halved

1 Combine spices in a medium bowl, add chicken; toss chicken to coat in mixture.

2 Cook lentils in a large saucepan of boiling water, uncovered, until just tender; drain. Rinse under cold water; drain. Place lentils in a large bowl with garlic, chilli, cucumber, capsicum, juice, oil and fresh coriander. Season to taste.

3 Meanwhile, cook chicken on a heated lightly oiled grill pan (or grill or barbecue) until browned both sides and cooked through. Add limes to pan; cook until browned. Serve chicken with lentil salsa and lime halves.

serving suggestion Accompany with mountain bread as the main course of a summer lunch.
tip If you like a lot of heat, you could add 1 teaspoon of harissa to the salsa instead of the chilli.

nutritional count per serving
▶ 17.1g total fat
▶ 4.5g saturated fat
▶ 2419kJ (578 cal)
▶ 32.4g carbohydrate
▶ 68g protein
▶ 12.5g fibre

While many Indian dishes involve long, slow cooking, this recipe captures the essence of the cuisine in a quick and easy char-grill.

chicken with kashmiri pilaf

PREP + COOK TIME 30 MINUTES (+ STANDING) **SERVES** 4

1 tablespoon vegetable oil

1 small brown onion (80g), chopped finely

1 clove garlic, crushed

1 teaspoon black mustard seeds

¼ teaspoon ground cardamom

½ teaspoon ground cumin

½ teaspoon garam masala

½ teaspoon ground turmeric

1½ cups (300g) long-grain white rice

3 cups (750ml) chicken stock

2 tablespoons coarsely chopped fresh coriander (cilantro)

⅓ cup (80g) mango chutney

2 tablespoons water

4 chicken breast fillets (800g)

1 Heat oil in a medium saucepan; cook onion, garlic and mustard seeds, stirring, until onion softens and seeds pop. Add remaining spices; cook, stirring, until fragrant.

2 Add rice; stir to coat in spices. Add stock; bring to the boil. Reduce heat; simmer, covered, until rice is just tender. Stir in coriander; cover to keep warm.

3 Meanwhile, combine chutney with the water in a small heated saucepan; cook, stirring, over medium heat until hot.

4 Cook chicken, brushing all over with chutney mixture, on a heated oiled grill plate (or grill or barbecue) until browned both sides and cooked through. Cut into thick slices. Serve chutney chicken with pilaf.

nutritional count per serving
- ▶ 17.2g total fat
- ▶ 4.5g saturated fat
- ▶ 2704kJ (646 cal)
- ▶ 70.9g carbohydrate
- ▶ 50.4g protein
- ▶ 1.6g fibre

test kitchen tips

Mango chutney will burn if the grill or barbecue is too hot. Accompany the chicken with some extra mango chutney, and a raita (finely chopped cucumber combined with low-fat yoghurt), if you like.

Couscous, the North African cereal made from semolina, lends an intriguing crunch to the coating on the chicken.

test kitchen tips

The salsa, without the avocado, can be prepared up to 3 hours ahead; store, covered, in the refrigerator. Add avocado just before serving. You could also add some coarsely chopped fresh coriander or finely chopped fresh chilli to the corn salsa. Accompany with steamed snow pea sprouts, if you like. For information on removing kernels from corn cobs, see page 112.

spicy couscous chicken with fresh corn salsa

PREP + COOK TIME 30 MINUTES **SERVES** 4

½ teaspoon ground cumin

¼ teaspoon ground coriander

¼ teaspoon garam masala

¼ teaspoon ground turmeric

½ cup (125ml) chicken stock

½ cup (100g) couscous

700g (1½ ounces) chicken breast fillets

1 egg white, beaten lightly

2 corn cobs (500g), trimmed

2 medium tomatoes (380g), seeded, chopped coarsely

1 small avocado (200g), chopped coarsely

2 tablespoons red wine vinegar

4 green onions (scallions), chopped finely

1 Preheat oven to 220°C/425°F.

2 Cook spices in a heated medium saucepan, stirring, until fragrant; add stock. Bring to the boil; stir in couscous. Remove from heat; stand, covered, about 5 minutes or until stock is absorbed, fluffing with fork occasionally.

3 Toss chicken in egg white; coat in couscous. Place chicken, in a single layer, in a large lightly oiled baking dish; bake, uncovered, in oven, for about 10 minutes or until chicken is cooked through. Cover to keep warm.

4 Remove kernels from corn cobs. Cook kernels in a small pan of boiling water, uncovered, for about 2 minutes or until just tender; drain. Rinse under cold water; drain. Combine corn with remaining ingredients in a medium bowl. Slice chicken thickly; serve with corn salsa.

nutritional count per serving
▶ 19.2g total fat
▶ 4.9g saturated fat
▶ 2191kJ (524 cal)
▶ 36.5g carbohydrate
▶ 47.4g protein
▶ 6g fibre

Tofu, also known as bean curd, is made from the 'milk' of crushed soya beans. Its fairly mild flavour is enhanced by the vegetables and sauce.

vegetable and tofu stir-fry

PREP + COOK TIME 25 MINUTES **SERVES** 4

500g (1 pound) fresh rice noodles

1 tablespoon peanut oil

1 large brown onion (200g), sliced thickly

2 cloves garlic, crushed

1 teaspoon chinese five-spice powder

200g (6½ ounces) button mushrooms, halved

200g (6½ ounces) swiss brown mushrooms, halved

¼ cup (60ml) soy sauce

1 cup (250ml) vegetable stock

¼ cup (60ml) water

300g (9½ ounces) baby buk choy, chopped coarsely

300g (9½ ounces) choy sum, chopped coarsely

4 green onions (scallions), chopped coarsely

250g (8 ounces) fresh firm tofu, cut into 2cm (¾-inch) cubes

1 cup (80g) bean sprouts

1 Place noodles in a large heatproof bowl, cover with boiling water; separate with a fork, drain.
2 Heat oil in wok; stir-fry brown onion and garlic until onion softens. Add five-spice; stir-fry until fragrant. Add mushrooms; stir-fry until almost tender.
3 Add combined sauce, stock and the water to wok; bring to the boil. Add buk choy, choy sum and green onion; stir-fry until buk choy just wilts. Add tofu and noodles; stir-fry until hot. Serve stir-fry topped with sprouts.

nutritional count per serving

▸ 10.4g total fat
▸ 1.6g saturated fat
▸ 1361kJ (325 cal)
▸ 35.3g carbohydrate
▸ 18.3g protein
▸ 7.9g fibre

test kitchen tip

You can use dried rice
stick noodles if fresh
noodles are not available.
Place dried noodles in a
large heatproof bowl;
cover with boiling water.
Stand until just tender,
then drain.

test kitchen tips

Passata is sieved tomato puree
available from supermarkets.
The flavour of the bolognese
will improve if it is made a day
ahead; reheat just before serving.

fettuccine bolognese

fettuccine bolognese

PREP + COOK TIME 30 MINUTES **SERVES** 4

1 small brown onion (80g), chopped finely

2 cloves garlic, crushed

1 small carrot (70g), chopped finely

1 stalk celery (150g), trimmed, chopped finely

400g (12½ ounces) lean minced (ground) beef

2 cups (500ml) passata

½ cup (125ml) beef stock

375g (12 ounces) fettuccine

1 Cook onion and garlic in a heated large non-stick frying pan, stirring, until onion softens. Add carrot and celery to pan; cook, stirring, until vegetables are just tender.

2 Add beef; cook, stirring, until beef is changed in colour. Add passata and stock; bring to the boil. Reduce heat; simmer, uncovered, about 15 minutes or until the mixture thickens slightly.

3 Meanwhile, cook pasta in a large saucepan of boiling water until just tender; drain.

4 Serve pasta topped with bolognese sauce.

serving suggestion A green salad and loaf of crusty ciabatta bread.

spaghetti with tomato and white bean sauce

PREP + COOK TIME 30 MINUTES **SERVES** 4

⅓ cup (80ml) vegetable stock

1 small red onion (100g), chopped finely

2 cloves garlic, crushed

1 cup (250ml) dry white wine

½ teaspoon caster (superfine) sugar

2 cups (500ml) passata

375g (12 ounces) spaghetti

1 tablespoon coarsely chopped fresh oregano

2 tablespoons rinsed, drained capers, chopped coarsely

½ cup (60g) pitted black olives, halved

400g (12½ ounces) canned butter beans, rinsed, drained

2 tablespoons coarsely chopped fresh flat-leaf parsley

⅓ cup (25g) shaved parmesan

1 Heat half the stock in a medium saucepan; cook onion and garlic, stirring, until onion softens. Stir in wine, remaining stock, sugar and passata; bring to the boil. Reduce heat; simmer, uncovered, until sauce thickens slightly.

2 Cook pasta in a large saucepan of boiling water until just tender; drain.

3 Meanwhile, add oregano, capers, olives and beans into sauce; stir until hot. Serve pasta with sauce; sprinkle over parsley and parmesan.

photograph page 84

nutritional count per serving
- 10.2g total fat
- 3.3g saturated fat
- 2310kJ (552 cal)
- 76.6g carbohydrate
- 33.9g protein
- 7.4g fibre

nutritional count per serving
- 4.5g total fat
- 1.8g saturated fat
- 2124kJ (507 cal)
- 84.9g carbohydrate
- 17.3g protein
- 8g fibre

test kitchen tip

Make the sauce a day ahead; store, covered, in the refrigerator. Beans are an Italian staple and are often served with spaghetti in the same dish.

spaghetti with tomato and white bean sauce (recipe page 83)

If you can't buy kaffir lime leaves, substitute the young leaves from any other citrus tree. Serve the fish parcels with lime cheeks or a salad made from fresh pomelo or grapefruit segments.

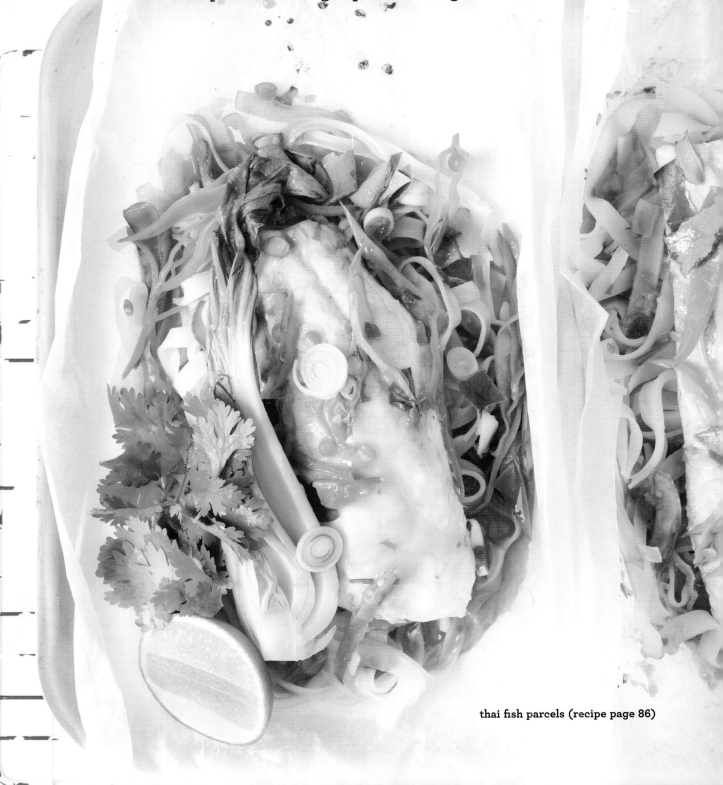

thai fish parcels (recipe page 86)

thai fish parcels

PREP + COOK TIME 25 MINUTES **SERVES** 4

200g (6½ ounces) dried rice stick noodles

4 x 150g (4½-ounce) bream fillets

150g (4½ ounces) baby buk choy, quartered

150g (4½ ounces) snow peas, sliced thinly lengthways

1 tablespoon thinly sliced lemon grass

8 kaffir lime leaves, torn

1 teaspoon soy sauce

2 tablespoons sweet chilli sauce

1 teaspoon fish sauce

2 tablespoons lime juice

1 tablespoon fresh coriander leaves (cilantro)

1 Preheat oven to 220°C/425°F.
2 Place noodles in a large heatproof bowl; cover with boiling water. Stand until just tender; drain.
3 Divide noodles into four equal portions; place each on a large piece of baking paper or foil. Top noodles with fish, buk choy, snow peas, lemon grass and lime leaves. Drizzle with combined sauces and juice. Enclose fish in baking paper or foil; place, on an oven tray.
4 Cook fish parcels about 15 minutes or until fish is cooked through. Place parcels on serving plates; open parcels, sprinkle with coriander leaves, and serve with lime cheeks, if you like.

tip Fish parcels can be assembled several hours ahead; store in the refrigerator.

photograph page 85

pesto fish kebabs

PREP + COOK TIME 25 MINUTES **SERVES** 4

600g (1¼ pounds) firm white fish fillets

1 tablespoon basil pesto

½ cup loosely packed, finely chopped fresh flat-leaf parsley

½ small savoy cabbage (600g), shredded finely

⅓ cup (65g) rinsed, drained baby capers

1 teaspoon finely grated lemon rind

½ cup loosely packed, finely chopped fresh mint leaves

1 Cut fish into 2cm (¾-inch) cubes; combine with pesto and 1 tablespoon of the parsley in a medium bowl. Thread onto 12 small skewers.
2 Cook kebabs, in batches, in a heated large lightly oiled frying pan until browned and cooked as desired. Cover to keep warm.
3 Add cabbage to same heated pan; cook, stirring, until just tender. Stir in remaining parsley, capers, rind and mint.
4 Serve fish kebabs on cabbage.

serving suggestion Lemon-scented steamed rice.
tip The fish can be marinated and threaded onto skewers a day ahead; store, covered, in the refrigerator.

---

nutritional count per serving

▶ 4g total fat
▶ 1g saturated fat
▶ 1271kJ (304 cal)
▶ 37.2g carbohydrate
▶ 35g protein
▶ 2.1g fibre

---

nutritional count per serving

▶ 5.5g total fat
▶ 1.5g saturated fat
▶ 920kJ (220 cal)
▶ 5.6g carbohydrate
▶ 3.7g protein
▶ 6.6g fibre

test kitchen tips

You can use any large fish fillets or steaks, such as ling, gemfish, snapper, kingfish or silver warehou, for this recipe. Soak 12 bamboo skewers in water for at least 30 minutes before using to avoid scorching or burning during cooking.

pesto fish kebabs

test kitchen tip

The fish cakes can be made in advance and frozen; defrost them in the refrigerator before cooking.

Redfish, usually sold skinned as fillets, is ideal for these fish cakes because of its delicate flavour. You can, however, use practically any mild-flavoured, skinless fish fillet.

thai fish cakes with noodle salad

PREP + COOK TIME 25 MINUTES **SERVES** 4

600g (1¼ pounds) firm white fish fillets, chopped coarsely

1 clove garlic, quartered

1 egg white, beaten lightly

⅔ cup loosely packed fresh coriander leaves (cilantro)

½ cup loosely packed fresh mint leaves

4 fresh small red thai (serrano) chillies, chopped finely

250g (4 ounces) rice vermicelli

2 teaspoons caster (superfine) sugar

¼ cup (60ml) lime juice

1 tablespoon sambal oelek

1 lebanese cucumber (130g), seeded, cut into matchsticks

100g (3 ounces) snow peas, sliced thinly

1 Blend or process fish, garlic, egg white and half the coriander, half the mint and half the chilli until mixture forms a paste; shape into 12 patties.

2 Cook patties, in batches, in a heated large non-stick frying pan until browned both sides and cooked through.

3 Meanwhile, place vermicelli in a large heatproof bowl; cover with boiling water. Stand until just tender; drain. Cover to keep warm.

4 Combine sugar, juice and sambal in a small saucepan; bring to the boil. Reduce heat; simmer, stirring, until sugar dissolves.

5 Combine remaining coriander, mint and chilli in a large bowl with vermicelli, sugar mixture, cucumber and snow peas; toss to combine.

6 Serve fish cakes on noodle salad.

serving suggestion Som tum, the Thai spicy-sour green pawpaw salad, is a good, low-kilojoule accompaniment to the fish cakes.

You can use any firm-fleshed white fish fillets for this recipe – we used blue-eye trevalla. Make the breadcrumbs from bread that is at least a day old; blend or process the stale bread to make the crumbs.

cheese-crumbed fish fillets with stir-fried vegetables

PREP + COOK TIME 35 MINUTES SERVES 4

1 cup (70g) wholemeal breadcrumbs

½ cup (45g) rolled oats

1 tablespoon rinsed, drained capers, chopped finely

2 teaspoons finely grated lemon rind

¼ cup (20g) finely grated romano cheese

¼ cup loosely packed, finely chopped fresh flat-leaf parsley

1 tablespoon sesame oil

4 x 150g (4½-ounce) firm white fish fillets

½ cup (75g) plain (all-purpose) flour

2 egg whites, beaten lightly

1 large carrot (180g), cut into matchsticks

2 stalks celery (300g), cut into matchsticks

1 medium green capsicum (bell pepper) (200g), sliced thinly

6 green onions (scallions), chopped finely

1 fresh small red thai (serrano) chilli, seeded, chopped finely

1 tablespoon sesame seeds

1 Preheat oven to 220°C/425°F.

2 Combine breadcrumbs, oats, capers, rind, cheese, parsley and oil in a medium bowl. Coat fish in flour, shake off excess; dip in egg white, then in breadcrumb mixture.

3 Place fish, in a single layer, in a baking dish; bake, uncovered, about 20 minutes or until fish are cooked through.

4 Meanwhile, stir-fry carrot in a heated wok. Add celery, capsicum, onion, chilli and sesame seeds; stir-fry until vegetables are just tender.

5 Serve fish with stir-fried vegetables; accompany with lemon wedges, if you like.

tip Fish can be crumbed several hours ahead; store, covered, in the refrigerator.

SNACKS

vegetable grill

PREP + COOK TIME 55 MINUTES   SERVES 4

2 large carrots (360g), chopped coarsely

2 tablespoons buttermilk

1 teaspoon each ground cumin and coriander

2 large red capsicums (bell peppers) (700g)

3 baby eggplants (180g), sliced thinly

1 small red onion (100g), sliced thickly

100g (3 ounces) button mushrooms, sliced thickly

200g (6½ ounces) canned artichoke hearts, drained, chopped coarsely

8 slices sourdough (320g)

1 cup (120g) coarsely grated low-fat cheddar

2 tablespoons coarsely chopped fresh flat-leaf parsley

1 Boil, steam or microwave carrot until just tender; drain. Blend or process carrot with buttermilk until smooth.

2 Cook spices in a small dry heated frying pan until fragrant (see page 113). Combine with carrot mixture; cover to keep warm.

3 Preheat grill (broiler). Quarter capsicums; discard seeds and membranes. Roast under grill, skin-side up, until skin blisters and blackens; cover capsicum pieces with plastic or paper for 5 minutes. Peel away skin (see page 112); slice capsicum thickly.

4 Cook eggplant, onion, mushrooms and artichoke, in batches, on a heated oiled grill plate (or grill or barbecue) until browned and just tender.

5 Toast sourdough on both sides.

6 Divide carrot mixture equally among toast slices; top with capsicum, eggplant, mushrooms and artichoke, sprinkle with cheese. Cook under hot grill until cheese melts. Sprinkle with parsley.

These between-meal snacks will satisfy
the heartiest of appetites – and your
waistline won't suffer for it.

nutritional count per serving
▶ 6.7g total fat
▶ 2.1g saturated fat
▶ 1935kJ (462 cal)
▶ 67g carbohydrate
▶ 26.9g protein
▶ 12.7g fibre

ham and asparagus grill

PREP + COOK TIME 20 MINUTES **SERVES** 4

340g (11 ounces) canned asparagus, drained

1 loaf turkish bread (430g)

2 medium tomatoes (300g), sliced

200g (6½ ounces) low-fat shaved ham

2 tablespoons coarsely chopped fresh basil leaves

1 small red onion (100g), sliced thinly

1 cup (100g) coarsely grated low-fat mozzarella

1 Preheat grill (broiler).

2 Place asparagus in a small bowl; mash with a fork until almost smooth.

3 Quarter bread; split pieces horizontally. Toast both sides.

4 Spread asparagus over toasts. Divide remaining ingredients among toasts, finishing with cheese; cook under hot grill until cheese melts.

nutritional count per serving
- 11g total fat
- 4.6g saturated fat
- 1830kJ (437 cal)
- 51.6g carbohydrate
- 28.8g protein
- 6.3g fibre

94

tuna and tomato toasts

PREP + COOK TIME 15 MINUTES **SERVES** 4

1 tablespoon rinsed, drained capers, chopped finely

2 teaspoons finely chopped fresh dill

2 teaspoons olive oil

2 tablespoons lemon juice

1 loaf turkish bread (430g)

4 medium tomatoes (600g), seeded, sliced thinly

4 green onions (scallions), sliced thinly

2 x 125g (4-ounce) cans smoked tuna slices in springwater, drained

1 Combine capers, dill, oil and juice in a small bowl.

2 Quarter bread; split pieces horizontally. Toast both sides.

3 Divide combined tomato and onion among toast slices; top with tuna, drizzle with caper mixture.

nutritional count per serving
- ▶ 7.3g total fat
- ▶ 1.5g saturated fat
- ▶ 1607kJ (384 cal)
- ▶ 51.9g carbohydrate
- ▶ 23.9g protein
- ▶ 4.9g fibre

95

DESSERTS

satsuma plum clafouti

PREP + COOK TIME 55 MINUTES SERVES 4

Sometimes called Indian blood plum, the large plum used in this recipe has a distinctive dark-red to purple fibrous flesh, is extremely juicy, pleasantly sweet, and is the plum most often found canned.

1½ cups (375ml) low-fat custard

¼ cup (35g) self-raising flour

1 egg yolk

2 egg whites

825g (1¾ pounds) canned whole plums, drained, halved, seeded

2 teaspoons icing (confectioners') sugar

1 Preheat oven to 180°C/350°F.
2 Combine custard, flour and egg yolk in a medium bowl.
3 Beat egg whites in the small bowl of an electric mixer on high speed until soft peaks form; fold gently into custard mixture. Pour into a 24cm (9½-inch) round ovenproof pie dish.
4 Pat plums dry with absorbent paper; arrange plums, cut-side down, over custard. Place pie dish on oven tray; bake, uncovered, about 40 minutes or until firm.
5 Just before serving, dust with sifted icing sugar.

serving suggestion Low-fat ice-cream.
tip Canned apricots or peaches can be substituted for the plums.

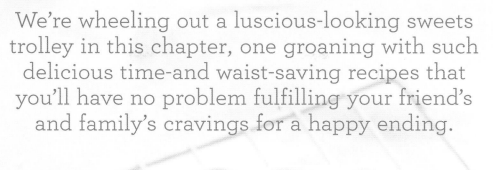

We're wheeling out a luscious-looking sweets trolley in this chapter, one groaning with such delicious time-and waist-saving recipes that you'll have no problem fulfilling your friend's and family's cravings for a happy ending.

nutritional count per serving
► 1.1g total fat
► 0.4g saturated fat
► 401kJ (96 cal)
► 18.5 carbohydrate
► 3g protein
► 0.7g protein

apple and cinnamon pancakes with maple syrup

PREP + COOK TIME 40 MINUTES   SERVES 4

1 cup (150g) self-raising flour

¼ cup (50g) brown sugar

½ teaspoon ground cinnamon

½ cup (125ml) skim milk

1 egg yolk

½ cup (110g) canned pie apple, chopped coarsely

2 egg whites

2 medium granny smith apples (300g), peeled, cored, cut into wedges

2 tablespoons brown sugar, extra

200g (6½ ounces) low-fat vanilla ice-cream

2 tablespoons pure maple syrup

1 Sift flour, sugar and cinnamon into a large bowl; stir in milk, egg yolk and canned pie apple.

2 Beat egg whites in a small bowl with an electric mixer on high speed until soft peaks form; fold gently into apple mixture.

3 Heat a medium non-stick frying pan over a medium-high heat; pour ¼-cup of the batter into pan; cook until browned both sides. Repeat with remaining batter to make a total of eight pancakes.

4 Cook apple wedges and extra sugar over a low heat in same pan, stirring, until apple caramelises.

5 Divide pancakes among serving dishes. Top with apple mixture then ice-cream; drizzle with syrup.

Pure maple syrup, the processed sap of the maple tree, has a natural affinity with apple. Maple-flavoured syrup or pancake syrup, made from cane sugar and artificial maple flavouring, is not an adequate substitute.

serving suggestion A flavoured ice-cream such as toffee crunch or butterscotch, can be used instead of plain vanilla; omit the maple syrup if you use a flavoured ice-cream.

nutritional count per serving
▶ 3.6g total fat
▶ 1.5g saturated fat
▶ 1544kJ (369 cal)
▶ 74.4g carbohydrate
▶ 10g protein
▶ 3g fibre

test kitchen tips

Any berry – boysenberries, blackberries, strawberries – can be substituted for the raspberries.
A pinch of grated nutmeg or ground cardamom can be added to the creamed rice mixture.

creamed rice with rhubarb and raspberries

PREP + COOK TIME 1¼ HOURS **SERVES** 4

1 litre (4 cups) skim milk
⅔ cup (150g) caster (superfine) sugar
½ cup (100g) medium-grain white rice
500g (1 pound) rhubarb trimmed, chopped coarsely
¼ cup (55g) caster (superfine) sugar, extra
200g (6½ ounces) raspberries

1 Combine milk and sugar in a medium saucepan; bring to the boil. Stir in rice; reduce heat. Simmer, covered, 50 minutes, stirring occasionally with a wooden spoon. Uncover; simmer 10 minutes or until rice is creamy and thickened.

2 Meanwhile, combine rhubarb and extra sugar in a large saucepan. Cook, stirring, over low heat, about 10 minutes or until rhubarb is tender.

3 Layer creamed rice and rhubarb mixture in serving dishes, finishing with rhubarb; sprinkle with raspberries.

nutritional count per serving
- ▶ 0.8g total fat
- ▶ 0.4g saturated fat
- ▶ 1782kJ (426 cal)
- ▶ 89.2g carbohydrate
- ▶ 13.5g protein
- ▶ 5.7g fibre

mocha self-saucing pudding

PREP + COOK TIME 55 MINUTES SERVES 4

1 cup (150g) self-raising flour

¾ cup (165g) caster (superfine) sugar

⅓ cup (35g) cocoa powder

2½ teaspoons instant coffee granules

½ cup (125ml) skim milk

1 tablespoon vegetable oil

½ cup (100g) firmly packed brown sugar

1¼ cups (310ml) boiling water

1 tablespoon icing (confectioners') sugar

1 Preheat oven to 160°C/325°F.

2 Sift flour, sugar, 2 tablespoons cocoa and 2 teaspoons of coffee granules into 1.25-litre (5-cup) overproof dish; gradually stir in milk and oil.

3 Sift brown sugar, remaining cocoa and remaining coffee evenly over flour mixture; gently pour the boiling water over brown sugar mixture. Bake pudding, uncovered, for about 45 minutes. Serve dusted with icing sugar.

serving suggestion Raspberries or blueberries and a scoop of low-fat ice-cream make a good accompaniment.

tip This pudding is best served hot because the sauce is quickly absorbed by the pudding.

nutritional count per serving

▶ 6.3g total fat
▶ 1.4g saturated fat
▶ 1830kJ (437 cal)
▶ 89.9g carbohydrate
▶ 6.7g protein
▶ 1.9g fibre

lemon cakes with passionfruit syrup

PREP + COOK TIME 35 MINUTES **MAKES** 8

1¼ cups (185g) self-raising flour

½ cup (110g) caster (superfine) sugar

2 teaspoons finely grated lemon rind

1 egg, beaten lightly

40g (1½ ounces) butter, melted

2 tablespoons skim milk

¾ cup (210g) low-fat yoghurt

1 cup (250ml) water

1 teaspoon cornflour (cornstarch)

½ cup (125ml) passionfruit pulp

2 tablespoons finely sliced lemon rind

1 Preheat oven to 180°C/350°F. Grease eight holes of a 12-hole (⅓-cup/80ml) muffin pan.
2 Combine flour in a medium bowl with ¼ cup of the sugar and all the grated rind. Add egg, butter, milk and yoghurt; stir until just combined. Divide mixture among pan holes; bake about 25 minutes. Stand cakes in pan 5 minutes before turning, top-side up, onto a wire rack.
3 Meanwhile, combine the water and remaining sugar in a small saucepan. Stir over heat until sugar dissolves; bring to the boil. Reduce heat; simmer, uncovered, without stirring, 10 minutes. Stir in blended cornflour and passionfruit until mixture boils and thickens. Strain into a small heatproof jug; reserve some of the seeds. Stir sliced rind and reserved seeds into syrup; cool. Serve lemon cakes with passionfruit syrup. Dust with icing sugar, if you like.

serving suggestion You could scatter a few berries, such as blueberries or raspberries, on each serving plate.
tip Lime rind can be substituted for the lemon rind.

nutritional count per cake
▶ 5.5g total fat
▶ 3.2g saturated fat
▶ 885kJ (211 cal)
▶ 33.6g carbohydrate
▶ 5.1g protein
▶ 3.1g fibre

You will need about six passionfruit to make this recipe.
The thin-skinned purple-black variety will yield much
more pulp than the thicker-skinned Panama passionfruit.

test kitchen tips

We used grand marnier, however, cointreau or triple sec can be substituted, or use your favourite citrus-flavoured liqueur. Navel oranges are ideal for this recipe because they have very few seeds.

caramelised oranges with ice-cream

caramelised oranges with ice-cream

PREP + COOK TIME 20 MINUTES **SERVE** 4

4 large oranges (1.2kg)

2 tablespoons brown sugar

2 tablespoons orange-flavoured liqueur

200g (6½ ounces) low-fat vanilla ice-cream

1 Preheat grill (broiler).
2 Peel oranges, removing as much white pith as possible; cut crossways into thick slices.
3 Place orange, in a single layer, on an oven tray. Sprinkle with sugar; drizzle with liqueur. Cook orange slices, both sides, under grill until just caramelised.
4 Divide ice-cream and orange slices among four serving dishes; drizzle with pan juices.

serving suggestion Sprinkle some finely chopped mint or purple basil over the oranges.

ricotta and berry trifles

PREP TIME 15 MINUTES (+ REFRIGERATION)
SERVES 4

125g (4 ounces) raspberries

125g (4 ounces) blueberries

200g (6½ ounces) strawberries, quartered

2 cups (480g) low-fat ricotta

⅓ cup (80ml) orange juice

⅓ cup (80ml) pure maple syrup

2 pavlova nests (20g) crumbled

1 tablespoon toasted flaked almonds

1 Combine berries in a medium bowl.
2 Blend or process ricotta, juice and syrup until mixture is smooth.
3 Divide half the ricotta mixture among four 1-cup (250ml) dessert glasses; sprinkle with meringue and half of the berries. Top with remaining ricotta mixture and berries.
4 Sprinkle nuts over trifles. Cover, refrigerate for at least 3 hours before serving.

serving suggestion Drizzle some pureed berries over the trifles.

photograph page 106

nutritional count per serving
▶ 1.8g total fat
▶ 1g saturated fat
▶ 905kJ (216 cal)
▶ 37.9g carbohydrate
▶ 4.6g protein
▶ 4.2g fibre

nutritional count per serving
▶ 12.4g total fat
▶ 6.9g saturated fat
▶ 1251kJ (299 cal)
▶ 31.3g carbohydrate
▶ 14.7g protein
▶ 3.7g fibre

test kitchen tips

The trifle can also be served in a large glass bowl. Pavlova nests are commercially made small meringue shells sold in packages of 10 at most supermarkets.

ricotta and berry trifles (recipe page 105)

test kitchen tips

Mousse can be prepared a day ahead; store, covered, in the refrigerator until just before ready to serve. We used Baileys Original Irish Cream, based on Irish whiskey, spirits and cream, in this recipe. Frûche is a commercial dessert having less than 0.5g fat per 100g; substitute fromage frais or a low-fat yoghurt if you cannot find it.

chocolate mousse (recipe page 108)

chocolate mousse

PREP TIME 10 MINUTES (+ REFRIGERATION) **SERVES** 4

2 teaspoons instant coffee granules

1 teaspoon hot water

120g (4 ounces) dark chocolate, melted

400g (12½ ounces) french-vanilla low-fat frûche

1 tablespoon irish cream liqueur

1 Combine coffee with the water in a medium bowl, stirring until coffee dissolves. Add chocolate, frûche and liqueur, stirring, until combined.
2 Divide mixture among four ¾-cup (180ml) serving dishes; refrigerate, covered, for about 30 minutes or until firm. Serve with berries, and dusted with sifted icing sugar, if you like.

serving suggestions Accompany mousse with raspberries, strawberries or blueberries.

photograph page 107

pineapple crunch

PREP + COOK TIME 30 MINUTES **SERVES** 4

840g (1¾ pounds) canned crushed pineapple, drained

2 small nashi pears (430g), chopped coarsely

1 tablespoon coconut-flavoured liqueur

1 cup (50g) Just Right cereal

1 tablespoon pepitas (dried pumpkin seeds)

1 tablespoon sunflower seeds

2 tablespoons low-fat yoghurt

1 tablespoon honey

1 Preheat oven to 180°C/350°F.
2 Grease four 1-cup (250ml) ovenproof dishes; place on an oven tray.
3 Combine pineapple, nashi and liqueur in a medium bowl; divide among dishes.
4 Combine cereal, seeds, yoghurt and honey in the same bowl. Divide mixture among dishes; bake, uncovered, about 20 minutes or until browned lightly.

serving suggestion Serve topped with low-fat yoghurt or low-fat ice-cream and a dollop of fresh passionfruit pulp or a drizzle of honey.

---

nutritional count per serving
- 9g total fat
- 5.3g saturated fat
- 1110kJ (265 cal)
- 32.9g carbohydrate
- 9.9g protein
- 0.4g fibre

---

nutritional count per serving
- 3.4g total fat
- 0.4g saturated fat
- 1085kJ (259 cal)
- 46.5g carbohydrate
- 4.6g protein
- 6.6g fibre

test kitchen tips

You can substitute chopped,
drained canned peaches or
apricots for the pineapple in
this recipe.

We used Just Right breakfast
cereal in this recipe but you
can use any flaked and dried
fruit cereal, even a muesli or
granola-like product.

We used Malibu liqueur but you
can use your favourite brand.

pineapple crunch

The best apple varieties to use for this recipe are granny smith and golden delicious as they hold their shape well.

apple and fig bread pudding

PREP + COOK TIME 1¼ HOURS **SERVES** 4

2 tablespoons honey

2 tablespoons water

8 slices white bread

1 medium apple (150g), cored, quartered sliced thinly

12 dried figs (200g), halved

2 cups (500ml) skim milk

2 eggs

2 tablespoons caster (superfine) sugar

¼ teaspoon ground cinnamon

2 teaspoons icing (confectioners') sugar

1 Preheat oven to 160°C/325°F.

2 Stir honey and the water in a small saucepan over low heat until combined.

3 Discard crusts from bread. Halve each slice diagonally; brush both sides of bread with honey mixture. Layer bread, apple and fig, overlapping pieces slightly, in a lightly greased shallow rectangular 1.25-litre (5-cup) ovenproof dish.

4 Whisk milk, eggs and sugar in a medium bowl; strain into a large jug, skimming and discarding any foam. Pour half the milk mixture over the bread; stand 5 minutes. Pour over remaining milk mixture; sprinkle with cinnamon.

5 Place dish in a large baking dish; add enough boiling water to come halfway up sides of baking dish. Bake pudding, uncovered, about 45 minutes or until top is browned lightly and pudding is set. Sprinkle with raspberries, if you like. Dust with sifted icing sugar before serving.

serving suggestion A dollop of low-fat yoghurt, flavoured with honey and cinnamon, or some fresh raspberries.

tip Remove bread and butter pudding from water bath immediately after cooking to prevent it from overcooking.

nutritional count per serving
- ▶ 4g total fat
- ▶ 1.1g saturated fat
- ▶ 1642kJ (385 cal)
- ▶ 72.7g carbohydrate
- ▶ 12.6g protein
- ▶ 8.8g fibre

COOKING TECHNIQUES

Washing leeks removes any grit from the inside layers. Cut in half lengthwise, stopping at the root. Fan the layers out and wash under fast-running cold water.

Rösti with ham and cherry tomatoes (1) (page 16), to make rösti, squeeze out the excess liquid from the grated potato. Mix the potato in a large bowl with the egg white. Divide the potato mixture into portions.

Rösti with ham and cherry tomatoes (2), spray a heated large frying pan with cooking-oil; add potato portions to pan, flatten with a spatula. Cook over medium heat until browned lightly and cooked through.

Palm sugar is usually sold in rock-hard cakes; use a fine grater to grate the palm sugar. If you can't find palm sugar you can use brown sugar, but palm sugar adds an authentic taste to Thai dishes.

To remove corn from fresh cobs, remove the husk (the outer covering) and the silk (the soft silky inner threads), and trim one side of the corn cob so it lies flat. Use a large flat-bladed knife to cut down the cob, close to the core, to remove the kernels.

To remove skin from a char-grilled capsicum, first roast the capsicum under a hot grill, skin-side up, until the skin blisters and blackens. Cover the capsicum with plastic or paper for 5 minutes, then peel away skin; slice capsicum as per recipe.

Crushing garlic Press unpeeled garlic firmly with the flat blade of a large knife (top) crushing the clove. Pull off the papery skin and chop the clove finely with the knife. A garlic press (bottom) removes and leaves the skin behind while crushing the garlic.

To use fresh thyme leaves, hold the top of the stem with one hand and run the fingers of the other hand down the stem to strip off the leaves. Any small, thin stems that break away with the leaves are fine to use.

Slicing ginger Cut the peeled ginger into thin slices then stack a couple of slices on top of each other. Cut lengthways through the stack to create matchstick-sized pieces.

Zesting citrus fruit A zester has very small, and very sharp, holes that cut the rind (the outermost layer of the fruit) into thin ribbons but leaves the bitter pith behind.

To chop fresh lemon grass cut 10cm (4 inches) up from the white end, or until you just reach the green part of the stalk. Discard the green section; cut the white part as finely as possible because lemon grass is so fibrous it doesn't soften during cooking.

To slice a capsicum, cut the top and bottom off and stand it on one end; slice down removing all the flesh. Discard the seeds and membranes, and slice the flesh according to the recipe.

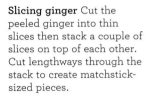

To make a thin omelette, lightly whisk the eggs, then pour into a heated lightly-oiled wok. Tilt the wok to cover the base with the egg; cook over a medium-high heat until the egg is set.

To julienne a carrot, is to cut it into matchstick-sized pieces. Cut the peeled carrot in half crossways, then into thin slices lengthways; cut the slices into thin matchsticks. You can trim the carrot into a rectangular shape, if you like; this will make it more secure on the cutting board.

Cutting an onion into wedges Cut the onion in half lengthways through the root. Remove the papery outer skin and trim the root end, but don't cut it off. Lie the onion cut-side down and cut the onion lengthways through the root into triangular-shaped wedges. The tiny piece of root at the end holds the wedges together.

Dry-frying spices releases their flavour and aroma. Dry-fry them over a medium heat, stirring constantly (and watch carefully to avoid burning) until the spices give off a warm aroma – remove from the pan as soon as the spices are fragrant so they don't burn.

GLOSSARY

ALL-BRAN a low-fat, high-fibre breakfast cereal based on wheat bran.

ALMONDS
blanched skins removed.
flaked paper-thin slices.
ground also known as almond meal; powdered to a flour-like texture.
paste we used almond-flavoured cake paste or prepared marzipan.
slivered small lengthways-cut pieces.

BACON RASHERS also known as slices of bacon; made from pork side, cured and smoked.

BAKING POWDER a raising agent consisting mainly of two parts cream of tartar to one part bicarbonate of soda (baking soda).

BARLEY FLAKES flattened grains produced by steaming the barley grain then rolling it into flakes.

BEEF
eye fillet tenderloin.
mince also known as ground beef.
rib-eye available as steaks or as whole pieces for roasting. A tender cut also known as scotch fillet.
rump steak boneless tender cut.

BEETROOT also known as beets.

BICARBONATE OF SODA also known as baking or carb soda.

BUK CHOY also called pak choi or chinese white cabbage; has a fresh, mild mustard taste. Baby buk choy is also available.

BREADCRUMBS
packaged fine-textured, crunchy, purchased, white breadcrumbs.
stale one- or two-day-old bread made into crumbs by blending or processing.

BURGHUL also known as bulghur wheat; hulled steamed wheat kernels that are dried and crushed.

BUTTER use salted or unsalted (sweet) butter; 125g equals one stick of butter.

CELERIAC ROOT vegetable with brown skin, white flesh and a celery-like flavour.

CHEESE
cheddar a semi-hard cows-milk cheese; we used a low-fat variety with a fat content of not more than 7%.
cream mild-flavoured fresh cheese made of cows milk; we used one with 21% fat.
fetta salty white cheese made from cows milk, though sheep- and goat's-milk varieties are available. We used low-fat fetta with 15% fat content.

mozzarella a soft, spun-curd cheese traditionally made from water buffalo milk; we used a version with 17.5% fat.
parmesan also known as parmigiano, parmesan is a hard, grainy cows-milk cheese originating in Italy. Parmigiano reggiano is generally aged longer than grana padano.
ricotta a low-fat, fresh unripened cheese made from whey with 8.5% fat.
romano hard sheep- or cows-milk cheese; straw-coloured and grainy in texture.

CHICKEN
breast fillet breast halved, skinned and boned.
mince also known as ground chicken.
tenderloin thin strip of meat lying just under the breast.
thigh fillet thigh from which the skin and bones have been removed.

CHICKPEAS also called garbanzos, hummus or channa; an irregularly round, sandy-coloured legume.

CHILLIES available in many different types and sizes. Use rubber gloves when chopping and seeding fresh chillies as they can burn your skin. Removing seeds lessens the heat level.
thai red also known as 'scuds'; tiny, very hot and bright red in colour. May also be sold as 'serrano' or 'bird's eye'.

CHINESE BROCCOLI also known as gai lum.

CHOY SUM also known as flowering bok choy or flowering white cabbage.

CIABATTA in Italian, the word means slipper, which is the traditional shape of this crisp-crusted white bread.

COCONUT MILK we used a canned light coconut milk with a fat content of less than 6%.

COOKING-OIL SPRAY we used a cholesterol-free cooking spray made from canola oil.

CORNFLOUR also known as cornstarch; used as a thickening agent in cooking.

CORNMEAL ground dried corn (maize); available in different textures.

COUSCOUS a fine, grain-like cereal product, made from semolina.

CURRY PASTES
masala literally meaning blended spices; a masala can be whole spices, a paste or a powder, and can include herbs and other seasonings. Traditional dishes are usually named after particular masalas.

tandoori consists of garlic, tamarind, ginger, coriander, chilli, spices and sometimes red food colouring.

EGGPLANT purple-skinned vegetable also known as aubergine.

FIVE-SPICE POWDER a fragrant mixture of ground cinnamon, cloves, star anise, sichuan pepper and fennel seeds.

FLOUR
buckwheat although not a true cereal, flour is made from its seeds. Available from health food stores.
plain a general all-purpose flour, made from wheat.
self-raising plain flour combined with baking powder in the proportion of 1 cup flour to 2 teaspoons baking powder.

FRUCHE commercial dessert with less than 0.5g fat per 100g. Similar to fromage frais.

GARAM MASALA a blend of spices, originating in North India; based on varying proportions of cardamom, cinnamon, cloves, coriander, fennel and cumin, roasted and ground together.

GINGER, FRESH also known as green or root ginger; the thick gnarled root of a tropical plant. Fresh ginger will keep, peeled and covered with dry sherry, in a jar in the refrigerator.

GOLDEN SYRUP a by-product of refined sugarcane; pure maple syrup or honey can be substituted.

GRAND MARNIER orange-flavoured liqueur.

HAM we used light ham which has a fat content of approximately 4% – about half that of regular leg ham.

IRISH CREAM we used Baileys Original Irish Cream, based on Irish whiskey, spirits and cream.

JUST RIGHT breakfast cereal containing wheat flakes, rolled oats, rye, sultanas and dried apricots.

KAFFIR LIME FRUIT medium-sized citrus fruit with wrinkly yellow-green skin, used in Thai cooking.
leaves aromatic leaves used fresh or dried in Asian dishes.

KUMARA Polynesian name of orange-fleshed sweet potato often confused with yam.

LAMB
cutlet small, tender rib chop.
fillet tenderloin; the smaller piece of meat from a row of loin chops or cutlets.

LAMINGTON PAN 20cm x 30cm slab cake pan, 3cm deep.

LAVASH flat, unleavened bread that originated in the Mediterranean.

LEMON GRASS a tall, clumping, lemon-smelling and -tasting, sharp-edged grass; the white lower part of each stem is chopped and used in Asian cooking.

LENTILS dried pulses often identified by and named after their colour; also known as dhal.

LOW-FAT CUSTARD we used custard with 0.9% fat.

LOW-FAT ICE CREAM we used an ice-cream with 3% fat.

LOW-FAT MAYONNAISE we used cholesterol-free mayonnaise with 3% fat.

LOW-FAT SOUR CREAM we used light sour cream with 18.5% fat.

LOW-FAT THICKENED CREAM we used thickened cream with 18% fat.

LOW-FAT YOGURT we used yogurt with a fat content of less than 0.2%.

MALIBU coconut-flavoured rum.

MAPLE SYRUP distilled sap of the maple tree. Maple-flavoured syrup or pancake syrup is made from cane sugar and artificial maple flavouring and is not an adequate substitute for the real thing.

MELONS
rockmelon oval melon with orange flesh; also known as a cantaloupe.
watermelon large green-skinned melon with crisp, juicy, deep pink flesh.
honeydew an oval melon with a delicate taste and pale-green flesh.

MESCLUN mixed baby salad leaves also sold as salad mix or gourmet salad mix; a mixture of assorted young lettuce and other green leaves.

MILK
buttermilk despite the implication of its name, is low in fat. Commercially made, by a method similar to yogurt. A good low-fat substitute for cream or sour cream.
skim we used milk with 0.15% fat content or lower.

MINCE also known as ground meat.

MUSHROOMS
button small, cultivated white mushroom having a delicate, subtle flavour.
swiss brown light to dark brown with a full-bodied flavour. Button or cup mushrooms can be substituted.

oyster also known as abalone; grey-white fan-shaped mushroom.

NOODLES
fresh rice thick, wide, almost white in colour; made from rice and vegetable oil. Must be covered with boiling water to remove starch and excess oil before using in soups and stir-fries.
hokkien also known as stir-fry noodles; fresh egg noodles resembling thick, yellow-brown spaghetti needing no pre-cooking before being used.
rice stick a dried noodle, available flat and wide or very thin; made from rice flour and water.

ONIONS
brown and white are interchangeable. Their pungent flesh adds flavour to a vast range of dishes.
green also known as scallion or (incorrectly) shallot; an immature onion picked before the bulb has formed, having a long, green edible stalk.
red also known as spanish, red spanish or bermuda onion; a sweet-flavoured, large, purple-red onion.

PAPPADUMS sun-dried wafers made from lentil and rice flours, oil and spices.

PARSLEY, FLAT-LEAF also known as continental parsley or italian parsley.

PASSIONFRUIT also known as granadilla; a small tropical fruit, native to Brazil, with a tough outer skin surrounding edible black sweet-sour seeds.

PATTY-PAN SQUASH also known as crookneck or custard marrow pumpkins; a round, slightly flat yellow to pale-green squash having a scalloped edge.

PECAN NUT native to the United States and now grown locally; golden-brown, buttery and rich.

PEPITAS dried pumpkin seeds.

PIDE also known as turkish bread, comes in long (about 45cm) flat loaves as well as individual rounds; made from wheat flour and sprinkled with sesame or black onion seeds.

PITTA (lebanese bread) also spelled pita, this wheat-flour pocket bread is sold in large, flat pieces that separate easily into two thin rounds. Also available in small thick pieces called pocket pitta.

POLENTA cereal made of ground corn (maize); is also the name of the dish made from it.

POPPING CORN a variety of corn that is sold as kernels. Available from most larger supermarkets.

PORK
fillet skinless, boneless eye-fillet cut from the loin.
mince also known as ground pork.
steak also known as schnitzel; thin slices cut from the leg or rump.

RAISINS large dried sweet grapes.

RHUBARB has thick, celery-like stalks that can reach up to 60cm in length. The stalks are the only edible portion of the plant – the leaves contain a toxic substance. Though rhubarb is generally eaten as a fruit, it is a vegetable.

RICE
arborio small, round-grain rice well-suited to absorb a large amount of liquid.
basmati a white fragrant long-grain rice.
brown natural whole grain.
calrose medium-grain rice; can be used instead of long- or short-grain varieties.
jasmine fragrant long-grain rice.
long-grain elongated grain, remains separate when cooked.
wild not a member of the rice family at all, but the blackish-brown seed of an aquatic grass native to the cold regions of North America. Wild rice has a strong nutty taste.

RICE FLAKES available from supermarkets and health food stores; also known as parva in India.

RICE PAPER SHEETS mostly from Vietnam (banh trang). Made from rice paste and stamped into rounds, with a woven pattern. They store well at room temperature, but are quite brittle and will break if dropped. Dipped in water, they become pliable wrappers for fresh (uncooked) vegetables.

ROLLED OATS, traditional whole oat grains that have been steamed and flattened. Not the quick-cook variety.

RYE FLAKES flat flakes of crushed rye grains.

SAUCES
barbecue a spicy, tomato-based sauce used to marinate or as a condiment.
char siu a Chinese barbecue sauce made from sugar, water, salt, fermented soya bean paste, honey, soy sauce, malt syrup and spices. It can be found at most supermarkets.

chilli we use a hot Chinese variety made from thai red chillies, salt and vinegar. Use sparingly, increasing the quantity to suit your taste.

fish also called nam pla or nuoc nam; made from salted pulverised fermented fish, usually anchovies. Has a strong taste and pungent smell.

hoisin a thick, sweet and spicy Chinese paste made from salted fermented soya beans, onions and garlic; used as a marinade or to baste foods.

kecap manis (ketjap) Indonesian sweet, thick soy sauce which has sugar and spices added.

oyster Asian in origin, this sauce is made from oysters and their brine, cooked with salt and soy sauce, and thickened with starches.

satay traditional Indonesian/Malaysian spicy peanut sauce served with grilled meat skewers. Make your own or buy one of the many packaged versions easily obtained from supermarkets or specialty Asian food stores.

soy made from fermented soya beans; several varieties are available in supermarkets and Asian food stores.
dark deep brown, almost black in colour; rich, with a thicker consistency than other types. Pungent but not particularly salty; good for marinating.
japanese an all-purpose low-sodium soy sauce made with more wheat content than its Chinese counterparts; fermented in barrels and aged. Possibly the best table soy and the one to choose if you only want one variety.
light a fairly thin, pale but salty tasting sauce; used in dishes in which the natural colour of the ingredients is to be maintained. Not to be confused with salt-reduced or low-sodium soy sauces.
tamari a thick, dark soy sauce made mainly from soya beans without the wheat used in standard soy sauce.
sweet chilli a comparatively mild, Thai-style sauce made from red chillies, sugar, garlic and vinegar.
teriyaki usually made from soy sauce, mirin, sugar, ginger and other spices; it imparts a distinctive glaze when brushed on meat to be grilled.
tomato also known as ketchup or catsup; a flavoured condiment made from tomatoes, vinegar and spices.
tomato pasta a prepared sauce made of a blend of tomatoes, herbs and spices.

Tabasco brand name of an extremely fiery sauce made from vinegar, hot red chillies and salt.
worcestershire made from garlic, soy sauce, tamarind, onions, molasses, lime, anchovies, vinegar and seasonings.

SESAME
seeds black and white are the most common of the oval seeds harvested from a tropical plant; however there are red and brown varieties also.
oil made from roasted, crushed, white sesame seeds; a flavouring rather than a cooking medium.

SOY WHOLEGRAIN FLAKES calcium-rich flakes made from soya beans.

SUGAR we used coarse granulated table sugar also known as crystal sugar, unless otherwise specified.
brown an extremely soft, fine granulated sugar retaining molasses for its characteristic colour and flavour.
caster also known as superfine or finely granulated table sugar.
dark brown a moist, dark brown sugar with a rich distinctive full flavour coming from natural molasses syrup.
demerara has a golden colour and subtle molasses flavour. The fine syrup coating on the sugar crystal, together with its coarseness, also gives a good colour to the crust of baking.
icing also known as confectioners' or powdered sugar; granulated sugar crushed with a small amount of cornflour.
palm very fine sugar from the coconut palm. It is sold in cakes, also known as gula jawa, gula melaka and jaggery. Palm sugar can be substituted with brown or black sugar.
pure icing also known as confectioners' sugar or powdered sugar. Has no cornflour, so is gluten free.
raw natural brown granulated sugar.

SULTANAS small dried grapes, also known as golden raisins.

SUMAC a purple-red, astringent spice ground from berries growing on shrubs that flourish wild in the Mediterranean; adds a tart, lemony flavour to foods.

TOFU also known as bean curd, an off-white, custard-like product made from the milk of crushed soya beans; comes fresh as soft or firm, and processed as fried or pressed dried sheets. Leftover fresh tofu can be refrigerated in water (which is changed daily) up to 4 days.

silken refers to a method by which tofu is made – where it is strained through silk.

TORTILLA unleavened bread sold frozen or fresh; made from wheat flour or corn (maize meal).

TRITICALE a nutritious hybrid of wheat (triticum) and rye (secale) which contains more protein and less gluten than wheat and has a nutty sweet flavour. Available in whole grain, flour and flakes.

UNPROCESSED BRAN made from the outer layer of a cereal, usually the husks of wheat, rice or oats.

VANILLA
bean dried long, thin pod from a tropical golden orchid grown in Central and South America and Tahiti; the minuscule black seeds inside the bean impart a luscious vanilla flavour.
extract made by extracting the flavour from the vanilla bean pod; the pods are soaked, usually in alcohol, to capture the authentic flavour. Imitation vanilla extract is not a satisfactory substitute.

VEAL
chop from the rib and loin (back).
steak thinly sliced cut also known as schnitzel.

VINEGAR
balsamic authentic only from the province of Modena, Italy; made from a regional wine of white Trebbiano grapes specially processed then aged in antique wooden casks to give the exquisite pungent flavour.
brown malt made from fermented malt and beech shavings.
cider (apple cider) from fermented apples.
red wine based on fermented red wine.
rice wine made from rice wine lees (sediment left after fermentation), salt and alcohol.
white made from spirit of cane sugar.
white wine made from white wine.

WHEAT GERM small creamy flakes milled from the embryo of the wheat.

WOMBOK also known as peking cabbage, chinese cabbage or petsai. Elongated in shape with pale green, crinkly leaves, this is the most common cabbage in South-East Asian cooking.

YOGURT, LOW-FAT we used yogurt with a fat content of less than 0.2%.

ZUCCHINI also known as courgette; small green, yellow or white vegetable belonging to the squash family.

INDEX

First published in 2001. Reprinted 2001, 2004 (twice), 2005.
This edition published in 2013 by Bauer Media Books, Sydney
Bauer Media Books is a division of Bauer Media Limited
54 Park St, Sydney
GPO Box 4088, Sydney, NSW 2001.
phone (02) 9282 8618; fax (02) 9126 3702
www.awwcookbooks.com.au

BAUER

MEDIA GROUP

BAUER MEDIA BOOKS
Publishing Director - Gerry Reynolds
Publisher - Sally Wright
Editorial & Food Director - Pamela Clark
Director of Sales, Marketing & Rights - Brian Cearnes
Creative Director - Hieu Chi Nguyen

Published and Distributed in the United Kingdom by Octopus Publishing Group
Endeavour House
189 Shaftesbury Avenue
London WC2H 8JY
United Kingdom
phone (+44)(0)207 632 5400; fax (+44)(0)207 632 5405
info@octopus-publishing.co.uk;
www.octopusbooks.co.uk

Printed by Toppan Printing Co., China

International foreign language rights, Brian Cearnes, Bauer Media Books
bcearnes@bauer-media.com.au

A catalogue record for this book is available from the British Library.
ISBN: 978 174245 376 7 (pbk.)

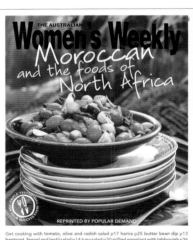